C000181450

Menopause

Mind the Gap

The value of supporting women's wellness in the workplace

Pat Duckworth

With

Victoria Howell and Jill McCulloch

Published by:

HWCS Publications

White House, Meeting Lane

Litlington

Royston, Cambs

England SG8 0QF

© 2020 Pat Duckworth

Cover Image and Design by Max Caddick

Editor Sarah Ross

The author has done her best to present accurate and up-to-date information in this book, but she cannot guarantee that the information is correct or will suit your particular situation.

Limit of Liability and Disclaimer of Warranty: The publisher has used best efforts in preparing this book, and the information provided herein is provided "as is".

Medical Liability Disclaimer: This book is sold with the understanding that the publisher and the author are not engaged in rendering any legal, medical or any other professional services. If expert assistance is required, the services of a competent professional should be sought.

This book is presented solely for educational and entertainment purposes. The author and publisher are not offering it as legal, accounting, or other professional services advice. While best efforts have been used in preparing this book, the author and publisher make no representations or warranties of any kind and assume no liabilities of any kind with respect to the accuracy or completeness of the contents and specifically disclaim any implied warranties of merchantability or fitness of use for a particular purpose. Neither the author nor the publisher shall be held liable or responsible to any person or entity with respect to any loss or incidental or consequential damages caused, or alleged to have been caused, directly or indirectly, by the information or programs contained herein. No warranty may be created or extended by sales representatives or written sales materials.

The legislation quoted in this book relates to the United Kingdom as at December 2020. The principles of making reasonable adjustments and taking a strategic approach to managing employees at menopause in the workplace are applicable worldwide.

Every company is different, and the advice and strategies contained herein may not be suitable for your situation. You should seek the services of a competent professional before beginning any improvement program.

Dedication

This book is dedicated to all the therapists, coaches, nutritionists, personal trainers, broadcasters, journalists and celebrities who have carried on talking about menopause and sharing their experiences to help to break the taboo of talking about this natural stage of life.

Here's what people are saying about
Menopause: Mind the Gap

"Talking about menopause in a workplace setting may feel uncomfortable but once you start that conversation you may be surprised how easy it can be. It's like pushing on an open door. And there are so many benefits for employers who embrace supporting women employees at this stage. This book gives you all the tools you need to start that conversation and create an inclusive workplace."

Sharon Livermore,
Director & Specialist Consultant at Kameo Recruitment Ltd

"Pat is the leading voice in educating the business arena worldwide on the fastest growing demographic in the workplace. She is pointing out clearly what a sustainable strategic approach to menopause can look like. In this insightful and practical book, you will find the way to create value and avoid the waste of underperformance, absenteeism and low morale. A must read for all managers that take inclusiveness serious."

Christine Koetsier,
Creator of Soul Language. Founder - Learn Your True Soul Language and Find the Roadmap to Your Life's Goal

"Menopause is not just about hot flushes. It also affects emotional and cognitive health. And there also valuable positive changes for women at this time of life. But it can be complicated and detrimental when one is navigating menopause (themselves or in the workplace) without compre-hension and facts. Pat Duckworth's book succinctly guides employers and managers through the steps of putting appropriate adjustments and strategies in place to benefit everyone."

Christine Powers,
Founder of Philosophers Camp

"When it comes to the workplace, talking about menopause is considered taboo even though it impacts your bottom line as a business. In her latest book, Pat Duckworth strategically shares the long-term impact of menopause on your workforce through under performance, lack of engagement and retention losses. Duckworth provides tangible solutions to handle this sensitive topic through training and resources. I highly recommend."

Dr. Shawne Duperon,
ShawneTV, Nobel Peace Prize Nominee.

"COVID-19 has shown that it is possible for companies to operate and grow while their staff enjoy flexible working conditions. Hopefully, this now marks major turning point for professional women experiencing natural life-cycle health challenges to be finally understood by their employers, and catered to within the workplace. The Future of Work has arrived and menopause can no longer be ignored."

Miriam Feiler,
Co-Founder Bizzi, Singapore

"Many companies overlook the impact of menopause on the wellbeing and performance of women employees. And yet research has shown that this oversight may be affecting profitability. Pat Duckworth sets out the business case for taking this issue seriously and gives you the practical steps for creating a profitable and inclusive working environment."

Teresa de Grosbois,
President Wildfire Workshops, Chair Evolutionary Business Council

"The most profitable companies and organizations put their people first and invest in their employees' health and wellbeing. Understanding the impacts of menopause and creating an inclusive workplace environment where the subject can be discussed openly enables your female employees to perform at their optimal level. Pat Duckworth is masterful at explaining why this subject is relevant in the workplace and how to engage in the right level of conversation. I highly recommend this book for all leaders."

Candy Barone,
CMCP, MBA, BSME, CEO & Founder You Empowered Strong (Y.E.S.) LLC

"Pat Duckworth's book is a must-read for employers seeking to build a diverse, transparent, and highly successful organization. It is a classic win-win-win. Employers have a clear-cut path to support women in menopause in ways that encourage them to take care of themselves, while finding their unique best way to navigate midlife challenges and be productive employees or leaders.

The author highlights simple, effective keys to help employers achieve transparency in the menopause conversation. These small actions are easy to implement, and potentially life-changing for the women. I highly recommend this book."

Dr. Lin Morel,
USA, Best Selling Author, Trauma and Stress Management Consulting since 1984

"Pat Duckworth offers practical insights into the nature of menopause, how it affects workplace performance and strategies for employers who are committed to supporting their employees at this stage of life. This is not 'one size fits all' and not only for women to understand. There are options for businesses of all sizes and structures."

Judy Van Niekerk,
Director at Judy Vee and Tribe of Traders

"Finally! A guide to help employers understand the impact of menopause in the workplace - and more importantly, the actions that will support female employees during transformative times. Pat Duckworth has provided organizations a pathway to not only supporting the wellness of women, but also to lead an era that recognizing the value of our most seasoned (and wise) workforce."

Lisa Dadd,
Business Leadership Strategist

"Whether you are an employer, an HR professional or a manager you need to be able to talk about menopause. The UK is leading the way on the subject of menopause in the workplace. Don't get left behind and find yourself in Employment Tribunal when with a few simple steps you could give your employees the support they need."

Teresa Wickham,
President at National Fruit Show

Contents

Foreword

In the past 30 years, since I joined the Fire Service, there have been major changes in the workplace – and that's a good thing. The Fire Service has become a more diverse and inclusive working environment. Just one aspect of that change is the number of women employed by the service now both as firefighters and back office support.

There is still room for improvement as we want to see more women at senior levels in the fire service. There are currently five female Chief Fire Officers in the UK.

Another ongoing change is that firefighters are staying with the service longer and into their 50s. This poses issues of staying fit and healthy to carry out duties for all operational officers. For women there are the additional challenges of dealing with menopause symptoms. That is not just the obvious hot flushes but also the less discussed symptoms such as anxiety, poor sleep, loss of confidence and brain fog.

Cheshire Fire Service believes that equality, diversity and inclusion underpins our approach to deliver an excellent emergency service as an employer. I am committed to creating an open workplace environment where these issues can be talked about freely and everyone can develop their talents.

To support this aim we created Limitless, a women's support network, and from that we have created a Menopause Policy. We have more plans for implementing the policy over the coming months. We want the policy to provide a framework and guidance that ensures the very best support for everyone dealing with any aspect of the menopause. Pat Duckworth has been instrumental in the development of this policy.

The foundation to a supportive approach to menopause lays in communication and knowledge. Pat Duckworth's work makes learning about menopause very accessible for everyone. It starts with helping people to understand menopause, the symptoms and the impacts. I have been privileged to see Pat Duckworth speak and to read this book. This has helped my organisation, my staff and me personally.

If you or your colleagues are not yet convinced that menopause is a workplace issue, Pat provides you with all the evidence you need to appreciate the potential impacts on your business. She goes on from there to let you know all the steps to providing the support people at menopause need, and the legal consequences of ignoring the issue.

If you want to create a diverse workforce that reflects your community and customers, the first thing you have to do is make it a safe place for your people to talk openly about personal issues without embarrassment or judgement. I am ready to talk about menopause – are you?

Mark Cashin, Chief Fire Officer,
Cheshire Fire and Rescue Service

Introduction

Change happens!

When I started work in 1972 women employees in the company automatically received 10% less pay than their male colleagues. That was normal practice at that time. Women didn't receive any maternity pay and there was an expectation that they would leave employment to bring their children up. It was not unusual for women to be sacked for becoming pregnant.

The Employment Protection Act 1975 was the first legislation in the UK that introduced maternity leave. The aim of this law was to protect the health of mothers and babies and to ensure a period free from excessive labour. Maternity leave rights were further extended in the 1980s and 1990s. In 2003 male employees received paid statutory paternity leave for the first time.

The Equality Act 2010 legally protects people from discrimination in the workplace and in wider society. It replaced previous anti-discrimination laws with a single Act, making the law easier to understand and strengthening protection in some situations. It sets out the different ways in which it's unlawful to treat someone. Employment Tribunal cases citing the Act have been successfully pursued by women experiencing menopause symptoms.

Women over the age of 50 are now the fastest growing demographic in the workplace. Some of that growth is a result of changes in maternity leave which have enabled women to stay in employment and build careers.

When I wrote my first book, 'Hot Women, Cool Solutions', in 2012 there was very little research and information available about the impact of menopause on women in the workplace. It was very forward thinking of my previous employers, HMRC, to invite me back in 2015 to speak to a mixed audience on Gender Equality Day about menopause. The men and women who attended had plenty of questions!

Since 2015 there has been recognition that women in their 40s and 50s experiencing menopause symptoms may need support in the workplace. In the 2019 UK General Election, the Labour Party manifesto promised radical changes to women's working rights including plans for a 'menopause policy' to force companies to address the needs of women at different stages in their lives.

Providing support in the workplace improves the health and wellbeing of women employees. There are also many positive results for employers. Research has shown that women who feel supported are more productive, take less sickness and absence leave and are less likely to leave their jobs. Taking a strategic approach to menopause in the workplace supports a culture of inclusivity, diversity and equality, and improves morale.

If businesses and organisations want to be viewed as good employers of women, it is essential to address their health and wellbeing needs at all stages of their lives.

This book is for employers who are committed to creating a supportive working environment for women at menopause. It provides information and guidance for managers, HR professionals, Equality and Diversity professionals, Occupational Health professionals, as well as for anyone who want to understand more about menopause.

Practical guidance on treatment options is also included so that this information can be shared with women colleagues.

Making changes to support women at menopause in the workplace does not need to be expensive. It starts with creating awareness around the issues and adopting an open and inclusive culture where menopause can be discussed without embarrassment.

This book generally adopts the term 'women' for those going through menopause. It also encompasses anyone with the biological set-up for menstruation who can experience menopause including transgender men, non-binary, and gender fluid people.

Case Study:
The Effect of Menopause Symptoms (Part 1)

Imagine for a moment a colleague. Let's call her Sam. She is in her mid-40s and has been with your business or organisation for a number of years. She has always been enthusiastic about personal development, training and advancing her career. She is a good team player, takes part in social events and is generally liked by her colleagues. Her good performance has been noticed and she has been earmarked for future promotion to a senior level. She is one of those employees that you would clone if you could.

Over a few weeks you start to notice that Sam is looking a bit tired. She is not chatting with colleagues as much as usual and seems to have less energy. You have a quiet word with her and ask her if she is okay. She says she has been having some problems with sleeping. Nothing is wrong. It's just a phase and she will get through it. She thanks you for asking.

During the next few months Sam doesn't seem to be getting any better. She's definitely quieter than usual. She's not contributing to team meetings in the way she used to. At her performance appraisal interview you mention it again. Her work output is still ok and there is no solid evidence that you can feedback to her. Sam is a bit defensive. She says that sleep is still a problem. She has tried taking over the counter remedies which provided some temporary relief. The doctor has given her some sleeping tablets but they make her feel worse during the day. She thinks it will pass. You let her know that your 'door is always open' and she can talk to you at any time.

Some weeks later, you are monitoring the Team's output figures and you notice that Sam's performance has deteriorated slightly. You make arrangements to have a one-to-one chat with her. You show her the figures and ask her if there is anything she would like to talk about. Is there a problem at home? She says she has been back to the doctor. The lack of sleep has left her feeling less clear-headed and it takes her longer to do her work. The doctor says that what she is describing are common symptoms of depression and he has prescribed a low dosage of antidepressants for her. She is reluctant to take them because she has always thought of herself as a cheerful, positive person but she can't go on feeling like this.

In the period up to the next appraisal, Sam's performance continues to deteriorate. She is quieter and more withdrawn. You have seen her having a nap at her desk during lunchtime. Her colleagues are commenting about it. You discuss performance with her. It is still just about at an acceptable level. Sam tells you that she is on a higher dosage of antidepressants. She is sleeping better but just has no energy or enthusiasm. You talk about the management training scheme to try to motivate her and she tells you that she doesn't even want to think about that this year or until she feels better.

This pattern of slow deterioration in performance and lack of engagement continues over the next eighteen months. You offer help and support but you are at a loss to know what is wrong.

One day Sam walks into your office and tells you that she is thinking of resigning.

To be continued....

This story was compiled from the experiences of a number of women I have worked with. When I tell this story at the beginning of workshops, women tell me that it was like hearing about their own experience. Men tell me that I am describing what they see in their partners.

Chapter 1

Why Menopause is a Workplace Issue

In recent years much more has been discussed about supporting women during menopause in the workplace. There have been several research studies and guidance notes prepared by various organisations including The Open University, Trade Union Congress (TUC), Chartered Institute of Personnel and Development (CIPD), and Faculty of Occupational Medicine (FOM), into the impact on women employees and organisations of menopause symptoms.

Women now make up nearly 50% of the workforce and there are more women over 50 in the workplace than ever before. In 2019, this was the fastest growing demographic not only in the UK workplace, but also in America and Australia. (Brewis, J. 2019). There are 61 million women over 50 in the US workforce (Harvard Business Review, Feb 2020). There are no statistics available yet for the impact of COVID-19 on these employment patterns.

Looking at the three months January to March 1993 compared with the same time frame in 2020, the labour market participation of women in the over 50 age group had increased by 21.2 percentage points. (Brewis, J. 2020)

There are many factors that influence more women to remain in the workplace over 50. On the positive side this includes improved opportunities to progress, and changed societal attitudes. On the negative side some women feel compelled to work longer because there is a gap in women's pension provision due to the gender pay gap and the changes in state pension provision.

It has been reported that of the 3.5million women over the age of 50 in employment in the UK, 75% report that they regularly experience menopause symptoms. As a result:

- 59% report difficulties that negatively affect their performance
- 52% say they have less patience with clients and colleagues
- 58% experience more stress
- 65% were less able to concentrate
- 30% have taken sick leave because of their symptoms (CIPD, 2019)

Similar issues have been observed in a new study of nearly 600 working women in Japan aged 45 to 65 years (NAMS, 2020). 'Researchers in the study found that a higher number of menopause symptoms were correlated with a lower work performance. More important, they found that working in an appropriate environment (one without high levels of stress) and maintaining a healthy lifestyle helped to reduce menopause symptoms. Conversely, they confirmed that women with numerous menopause symptoms were more likely to report a lack of exercise, chronic disease, and job-related stress.'

Women are often reluctant to talk with their managers about symptoms that are having a detrimental impact on their performance due to embarrassment and to a perception of prejudice against older workers. The ease of the conversation depends on the culture within the organisation and the attitude of the manager (see Chapter 4). It does not matter whether the manager is male or female, young or old.

Menopause symptoms can affect women at any level within an organisation but it can be particularly difficult for women in senior leadership roles to talk about. They may feel that it will undermine their authority and their opportunities for progression. Dr Elizabeth Farrell, medical director at Jean Hailes for Women's Health in Australia, says, "There's a sense that somehow it will diminish their capacity to function or demean them. I think that the education of men and women about the expectations of what will happen when periods stop, and the time leading up to it, is incredibly important." (Australian Financial Review, Feb 2020).

Despite the challenges of menopause there are many positive aspects. Firstly, there is the freedom from monthly menstrual cycles which can be very debilitating. The focus can move away from concerns about reproductive issues. This is also a stage when childcare responsibilities are reducing and women have more time for their career and achieving their potential. It is like a cognitive re-boot where women can use all the knowledge and experience, they have accumulated.

Advantages of providing support

Employers who support women colleagues at menopause can achieve:

- improved productivity,
- reduced sickness leave and absenteeism,
- better staff retention

- higher morale
- improved employee relations
- a more diverse and inclusive culture
- active social responsibility
- recognition as a good employer.

Supporting women colleagues at menopause with solutions such as tailored absence policies, flexible working patterns, and low-cost environmental changes can be simple and highly effective.

Women who were supported in the workplace from their managers and colleagues reported that it was 'considerably valued'. 'They believed it enabled them to continue working well and productively.' (Griffiths et al 2010).

A major benefit to employers of taking a strategic approach to menopause and putting supportive policies in place is about corporate social responsibility. Enhancing the wellbeing of employees is not only a 'good thing' to do, it also means that the organisation will be seen as an exemplar of a good employer of women. This can lead to business awards and the ability to attract more women to the organisation as employees and customers.

The cost of not providing support

On the negative side, employers who ignore this issue make themselves vulnerable to Employment Law cases. There is employment legislation that can be applied to employees experiencing menopause symptoms. There have been several cases successfully brought by women experiencing long-term symptoms that have had a severe adverse effect on their work activities (see Chapter 8).

Approximately 20-25% of women experience disruptive menopause symptoms. A 2013 survey of 900 women in managerial and administrative occupations (Griffiths, A. 2013) found that problematic symptoms included: lowered confidence, poor concentration, and poor memory.

There are no accurate statistics for the financial impact on businesses of menopause in the workplace. A report published in 2017 (Brewis, J. 2017) considered that many of the costs of women's economic participation during menopause transitions are borne by women themselves. This can take the form of them voluntarily reducing their working hours, taking less stressful, lower paid jobs, or withdrawing from the workplace completely.

The Report, using a conservative estimate of over 174,000 women in the workplace experiencing symptoms that affect their ability to work, concluded that:

"The absence of these 174,200 women aged between 50 and 54 cost the economy at least £7.3million in absence-related costs… but this estimate failed to include other costs like "symptom-related lateness for work, lost productivity due to medical appointments during working hours [and] women who reduce their working hours due to symptoms".

Another issue in the workplace is the retention of experienced women employees. In one survey, 25% of women reported that they considered leaving work because of their symptoms. No statistics are available for the number of women who actually left.

The costs of recruitment and replacement are not inconsiderable. A report by Oxford Economics in 2014 (HR Review) estimated that the cost of replacing a member of staff on a salary of £25,000 was £30,614. This includes the cost of recruitment and the cost of lost output while training a new employee.

The business case for supporting women at menopause in the workplace is clear.

The only question is: what scale of support is suitable for your organisation?

For book bonuses go to http://www.patduckworth.com/menopausemindthegap

Chapter 2

Understanding the Basics of Menopause
What is Menopause?

M enopause is not an illness. It is a stage of life, just like puberty, where major changes are occurring to the reproductive hormones giving rise to physical, mental and emotional effects.

The term menopause is often used to refer generally to the years of women's lives either side of their last menstrual period. It is more technically correct that menopause is the day one year after the last menstrual period. It is sometimes called 'the change' or 'time of life'. For more terms and definitions see Appendix 1- Definitions.

Naturally occurring menopause can take place as early as 40 or not until 55 but the average age is 51. Menopause that occurs before the age of 40 is known medically as 'premature ovarian failure' (POF) or 'primary ovarian insufficiency' (POI).

Symptoms start during the stage known as 'perimenopause'. Perimenopause refers to the years either side of the last menstrual period when the reproductive hormones are reducing.

Although most women who experience menopause symptoms only do so for between two to eight years, some women continue to have symptoms, particularly night sweats, into their 60s and 70s.

For most women the progress towards menopause takes place gradually over a number of years but some women experience a 'cliff edge menopause'. In those cases, women have a sudden and dramatic onset of symptoms.

Men can experience some menopausal type symptoms as their hormone levels change in later life. This period is known as 'andropause'. Men produce less testosterone after the age of 40. This can lead to hot flushes, lethargy, mood swings, irritability, and decreased sexual desire.

Some of these symptoms may affect men's performance in the workplace. (See Appendix 5 Men at Midlife – Male Menopause)

Medical Menopause

Women may experience menopause at any age due to medical treatment. This includes:

1. Hysterectomy

Hysterectomy is a surgical process to remove the womb (uterus). All hysterectomies involve the removal of the womb but may also involve cervix, ovaries, fallopian tubes, ovaries, lymph glands, and fatty tissue.

The type of hysterectomy performed will depend on the reason for the surgery.

In pre-menopausal women, if the ovaries are removed during hysterectomy, the women will go through menopause. This is referred to as a 'surgical menopause' and women will generally be offered hormone replacement therapy to mitigate the menopause symptoms and possible health complications such as low bone density (osteoporosis), and heart health issues.

Hysterectomy is the second most common surgery performed on women with 56,976 performed in UK NHS hospitals in 2011/2012 (healthyhappywoman.co.uk) and over 500,000 hysterectomies performed in the United States every year (hysterectomy.org). The number of hysterectomies being performed is decreasing year on year as new treatments for gynaecological issues are implemented.

2. Treatment for cancer

One of the main treatments for hormone receptor-positive breast cancer is hormone therapy. Hormone therapy lowers the levels of oestrogen or progesterone hormones to stop their stimulating effect on cancer cell growth.

In pre-menopausal women hormone treatment can give rise to menopause symptoms, particularly hot flushes and night sweats.

3. In Vitro Fertilisation (IVF)

IVF is one of several techniques available to help people with fertility problems.

There are various IVF protocols and they can vary greatly in the amount of time taken. Often the first stage of the IVF process is to suppress the woman's natural menstrual cycle using medication. This is like a medically induced menopause and can give rise to hot flushes and headaches (see Appendix 1).

4 Transgender Menopause

Transgender men identify as male but were assigned female at birth. Transition may take the form of hormone treatment and/or surgery. Hormonal treatment with testosterone to promote male physical characteristics decreases the production of oestrogen. This will give rise to cessation of periods and some menopause symptoms in pre-menopausal subjects.

Pre-menopause trans men who proceed to surgical menopause by having the ovaries and uterus removed will experience menopause symptoms. This may happen at an earlier age than commonly happens with a natural menopause. It can lead to other health complications including the risk of osteoporosis, raised blood pressure, and heart health issues.

Transgender men who do not take any action to transition medically will go through menopause in the usual age range.

Transgender women identify as female but were assigned male at birth. Transitioning usually involves taking oestrogen and then progressing to reassignment surgery. Trans women may experience symptoms similar to having periods but without the bleeding. They may experience pseudo-menopausal symptoms if their hormone therapy treatment is interrupted or levels are unstable.

'Trans people report that for those with unstable hormone levels, access to local services that responsively and proactively monitor and manage hormone levels is currently lacking. As such, many trans people are likely to experience at least some menopausal symptoms.' (TUC, 2017)

Factors Affecting the Experience of Menopause

There are a number of factors that can affect the nature of the menopausal symptoms that women experience. The main factors are:

Genetics. One predictor of menopause experience is what happened to close female relatives, such as mother or sisters, during their menopause. Their experiences can give a clue to the timing and symptoms that might be expected. However, every woman's experience of menopause is unique and genes are only one factor.

Nutrition. Food provides the building blocks for our bodies and contributes not just to our physical body but also to emotional make-up and cognitive powers. The quantity and quality of a woman's nutrition will influence the nature of her perimenopause.

Lifestyle. There are a number of lifestyle factors that have been shown to affect menopausal symptoms including exercise, smoking, recreational drugs, and drinking alcohol.

Stress. Stress causes the release of the hormones cortisol and adrenaline into the blood system. These inflammatory hormones can exacerbate menopause symptoms giving rise to more frequent hot flushes, poor sleep, anxiety, and weight gain.

Mindset. A positive approach to menopause coupled with support at home and at work has been shown to lessen the experience of menopause symptoms.

Underlying medical conditions. The changes in hormone levels may aggravate existing health issues.

Support. Women who are supported during menopause both at home and in the workplace, report feeling less impact from menopause symptoms.

There is also research that shows evidence of cultural differences affecting the experience of menopause. This can be linked to the status of older women in society.

Hormonal Changes

As women come towards the end of the reproductive stage of their lives, their supply of eggs reduces and the levels of hormones associated with reproduction begin to decline. This results in the end of menstruation and gives rise to physical changes in the body.

The reproductive hormones involved are:

Oestrogen – Commonly thought of as the 'female hormone', although men produce small quantities of it too, it helps to develop the female sexual characteristics, and, as a growth hormone, increases bone formation, supports brain function, and protects the heart as well as helping to improve mood.

Progesterone – The key hormone in pregnancy, it helps to maintain pregnancy and prevents further fertilisation. It is this hormone that triggers the menstrual bleed. It also has an impact on mood.

Testosterone – Small amounts of testosterone are produced by women in the ovaries and adrenal glands. Not much is known about the role of testosterone in women, but scientists believe it helps to maintain muscle and bone strength, and contributes to confidence, and libido.

The gradual decline in the reproductive hormones also impacts on the operation of the other major hormones in the body:

Insulin. Insulin helps to move glucose from the blood into the cells for use as energy. Oestrogen is important in optimising the insulin response in cells. During perimenopause insulin levels go higher. This can lead to glucose being stored as fat and it can be a precursor to Type 2 diabetes

Triiodothyronine (T3). The thyroid gland produces two hormones: thyroxin (T4) and triiodothyronine (T4). T3 is biologically active and influences the activity in practically every system in the body: metabolic rate, blood pressure, breathing, digestion, and nerve function. The reduction in the reproductive hormones can lead to an underactive or overactive thyroid.

Adrenaline and Cortisol. The adrenal glands produce adrenaline and cortisol. These two hormones work together to speed up heart rate, regulate blood pressure and aid other bodily functions to deal with stress. Oestrogen and progesterone help to regulate the production of cortisol. Menopause can lead to heightened levels of anxiety and adrenal fatigue.

Menopause Symptoms

Common physical symptoms that may affect performance at work include:
- Poor or interrupted sleep
- Hot flashes/Night sweats
- Lack of energy
- Dizziness or faintness
- Headache/Migraine
- Irregular/heavier menstrual periods
- Heart palpitations

Emotional and cognitive symptoms may include:
- Anxiety
- Mood swings
- Depression
- Forgetfulness
- Brain fog
- Loss of confidence
- Low mood

Many women enter perimenopause with limited knowledge of what they might experience. It is not a subject that is included in the school curriculum and is not a common topic of conversation among younger women.

In the initial stages of perimenopause, symptoms may be irregular and mild and they often go unnoticed. If they become more regular and intense, they will start impact on the woman's life and performance. However, symptoms such as poor sleep, anxiety, and mood swings may be interpreted as having other causes such as insomnia or depression. This can lead to misdiagnosis and inappropriate treatment.

Feelings of anxiety and loss of confidence can develop slowly and are often connected to poor quality sleep.

Hot flushes are one of the most commonly recognised symptoms of menopause. The experience of hot flushes varies from a feeling of hotness that lasts for about a minute to a distressing episode of heart palpitations, intense heat, and profuse sweating followed by shivering that can last up to five minutes.

Options for treatment

The options for treating menopause symptoms can be divided between medication, complementary therapies, and lifestyle changes (see Appendix 2).

The specific medication to help balance and supplement the reproductive hormones is Hormone Replacement Therapy (HRT) which comes in many forms and combinations. Doctors and Specialists may also prescribe for specific symptoms such as depression, anxiety, insomnia, osteoporosis, and hypertension.

The global market for women's health care is projected to grow from in $9.6 Billion 2019 to $17.8 Billion in 2024 (re: Jerusalem, 2020) indicating the extent of the issue and the market.

There is a range of complementary therapies to support women at menopause such as:

1. Mind/body techniques - Hypnotherapy, Cognitive Behavioural Therapy, Meditation, and Counselling
2. Physical therapies - Acupuncture, Reflexology, and Massage.

3. Herbal remedies and food supplements – Agnus Castus, Evening Primrose, Black Cohosh, Sage, St John's Wort, vitamins, and minerals

4. Other – Homeopathy, Aromatherapy

Lifestyle changes that can increase wellness and reduce symptoms include reviewing nutrition, exercise, and habits.

For Book Bonuses http://www.patduckworth.com/menopausemindthegap

Chapter 3

Recognising the Impact on Performance and Profitability

The impact on organisations of employees experiencing frequent and/or intense menopause symptoms in the workplace has been shown to include:

- Impaired performance
- Increased sickness leave
- Absenteeism/Presenteeism
- Lower morale
- Loss of confidence
- Early departure and

- Employment Tribunal Cases

How symptoms affect work place performance

The impact on workplace performance of some symptoms can be readily understood.

1 Poor Sleep

A common symptom of menopause is poor sleep. This can be the result of hormonal changes leading to night sweats, stress, anxiety, and weight gain.

A woman experiencing prolonged periods of reduced or poor-quality sleep will start to experience a range of secondary symptoms. Initially she will experience tiredness and a loss of energy. If the sleep issue continues it is likely to lead to cognitive issues such as brain fog, memory problems, and forgetfulness. It may also lead to emotional symptoms such as anxiety and low mood.

Ability to perform tasks will be affected by poor sleep and the secondary symptoms arising from it. Tasks may be performed with less accuracy or the volume of work may reduce.

Women in senior leadership or management roles may find that they become less articulate because they forget words when under pressure. They may also find the clarity of their thinking or problem solving affected.

If this problem is identified and continues it can be alleviated by negotiating changes in working hours or flexible working where that is appropriate to the organisation (See Chapter 5 Making reasonable adjustments)

2 Hot Flushes

Hot flushes are the most recognisable and noticeable symptom of menopause. They are a vasomotor response to the hormonal changes. Approximately 75% of women experience hot flushes and/or night sweats although for many they may be mild and of short duration.

There are many triggers for hot flushes including: stress, embarrassment, ambient temperature, dehydration, hot drinks or food, and clothing made from man-made fabrics that inhibit natural heat loss.

For women experiencing regular and intense hot flushes the impact on their workplace performance will depend on the nature of their role. I worked with a woman client who was employed in a jeweller's shop. Following a hot flush, she sweated profusely which reacted with the silver items turning them black.

Women who are required to wear a uniform at work may need changes to items of clothing particularly if it covers pulse points such as the neck, wrists, and elbows. Manmade fibres exacerbate the problem.

Most women feel embarrassed by hot flushes because they are so visible and can be interpreted as nervousness or anxiety. This can lead to the sufferer withdrawing from situations that might trigger a flush such as direct contact with customers, speaking up at meetings, or giving presentations. That type of avoidance behaviour can have a serious impact on women's progression at work.

3 Anxiety

Research carried out in 2013 (Fineberg et al) estimated that there were 8.2 million cases of anxiety in the UK. In England women are almost twice as likely to be diagnosed with anxiety disorders as men. Lost productivity due to anxiety was the largest component of the economic cost of these disorders which is estimated at £9.8 billion a year.

Women can experience higher levels of anxiety during perimenopause. This may be due to poor sleep or the impact in the reduction of the reproductive hormones on the production of adrenaline and cortisol.

This stage of life is particularly busy for many women as their children get ready to leave home, older parents need more help and support, and work becomes more challenging. These circumstances can increase stress levels and give rise to anxiety.

Symptoms of anxiety include: faster heart rate, dizziness, headaches, chest pains, loss of appetite, inability to relax, tearfulness, feeling tense, and poor sleep.

Women who are not supported or ignore the early signs of anxiety can go on to experience panic attacks or adrenal fatigue.

Episodes of anxiety not only affect productivity, but they may also lead to lengthy periods of absence. Early identification of the issue, intervention, and support can avoid these costs.

4 Low mood and depression

Just as with anxiety, women can be more susceptible to low mood and depression at perimenopause due to the reduction in the reproductive hormones. Women who have previously experienced depression are more prone to it at menopause.

Depression and menopause share many similar symptoms including poor sleep, fatigue, anxiety, and difficulty concentrating. This can lead to misdiagnosis with menopause being diagnosed as depression and vice versa. (Stewart,2019).

Low mood and depression can also lead to low self-esteem and reduced motivation, both of which will impact on performance at work.

5 Fatigue

A feeling of fatigue is a common symptom reported by women at menopause. This may arise at menopause from poor or interrupted sleep but can also be due to thyroid dysfunction, anaemia, depression or anxiety.

Fatigue is not just tiredness. It can be experienced as a lack of energy and motivation. It may also be associated with aching limbs and joints. The feeling of fatigue can lower resilience, making it harder to bounce back from challenging situations or illnesses.

This type of fatigue should not be confused with adrenal fatigue or chronic fatigue syndrome which both require medical intervention.

An employee experiencing fatigue will find routine day to day activities strenuous and exhausting. The sufferer can become easily overwhelmed.

It is easy to imagine the impact on an employee of periods of fatigue. It will affect performance, output and morale and may result in absenteeism or presenteeism.

For Book Bonuses http://www.patduckworth.com/menopausemindthegap

Chapter 4

Handling Sensitive Conversations

It is not surprising that several studies have shown that women are reluctant to discuss menopausal health issues that are affecting their attendance at work or their performance. They find it embarrassing or are concerned that their manager will become embarrassed.

In research carried out by CIPD (2019) 45% of women who said they could not talk about menopause with their manager cited privacy as their main concern. 34% said embarrassment was the issue and 32% said an unsupportive manager was the reason.

In addition, research by Hult Ashridge (2019), where 5,000 employees worldwide were surveyed, found that, 'Fear tends to stop females from speaking up more than their male colleagues, particularly; fear of being perceived negatively, fear of upsetting others and lack of confidence in their own views. The percentage difference between females and males on these items are 11%, 8% and 11% respectively. One theme that emerges in the qualitative data is the fear of looking or feeling silly.'

Women are also concerned that menopause symptoms are a sign of ageing which can have a negative impact on career progression opportunities.

The exceptions to this reluctance to speak up occur in organisations that have a diverse workforce and are where menopause is openly discussed. There will be less embarrassment where a manager has shared personal experiences of their own or a family member's menopause with colleagues.

Female staff will feel encouraged to talk about what they are experiencing and seek support if their manager has regular conversations that include asking about their general wellbeing and they share information about workplace events which relate to menopause, wellbeing and diversity.

A conversation between a manager and a female colleague about menopause could arise in several ways, such as:

- A female colleague instigating the conversation in order to seek support
- A conversation following a female colleague returning to work after sickness absence
- A discussion about performance
- An appraisal interview where underperformance has become an issue

The subject of menopause may also arise between a male or female colleague and his/her manager where a partner has been adversely affected by symptoms and it is having an impact on them. This can occur where a partner's sleep has been disrupted or they are experiencing high levels of anxiety or low mood.

A discussion about performance should not appear to come out of the blue for an employee. Regular feedback is a staple of good management. It is essential to have those informal conversations if changes in an employee's behaviour or performance have been noticed so that a small issue does not become a big problem. Being seen as approachable and easy to talk to is more likely to yield good results.

A woman employee is not required to talk about her menopause and it would be a mistake to ask a direct question about it if the employee has not raised it.

Seven Steps to Effective Conversations

1 Be Prepared

To get a good outcome from the conversation for all the parties, it is not enough to have good intentions. Employee issues concerning poor performance, personal problems, complaints and reassurance may be uncomfortable but for line-managers or managers in a small organisation, this is generally something that needs to be dealt with.

There may be a reluctance to get involved in what might appear to be a personal issue but, if this conversation is avoided, the employee may take more sickness absence leave, work less efficiently, cause lower morale in the team or instigate a grievance procedure. There is even the risk of losing an experienced and valuable member of staff.

Once this responsibility has been accepted by the manager, preparation is required to establish the right environment, acquire basic knowledge, set clear boundaries, and develop communication skills.

If the manager is busy when they are approached by a female employee for a conversation about her health or performance, they may not feel able to give her the time and attention she needs in that moment. They should check if it is urgent and, if not schedule, a date and time that is suitable for both parties. It is important not to appear to be dismissing the issue by rushing it. After all, it may have taken the employee a long time to build up the courage to raise it.

2 Environment

If this is going to be a frank and open one-to-one conversation, an appropriate location should be organised that will facilitate it. It needs to be somewhere that the conversation will not be disturbed by telephone calls, incoming emails or other colleagues. Unless there is a particularly good reason not to, both people should turn off mobile phones to avoid distraction.

Think about the layout of the room and what is appropriate to the nature of the meeting. Sitting across a desk or table from someone is very formal and is usually appropriate for performance reviews. Sitting at ninety degrees to each other can feel more relaxed and more suitable for discussions about personal issues and health.

Make sure there is drinking water available and paper tissues may be needed.

When booking a suitable space, allow enough time to discuss the issues.

3 Basic Knowledge

A basic understanding of menopause, the symptoms, the effects and the possible treatments will enable the manager to understand the terms the employee may use to refer to it. It is inappropriate to provide medical advice or suggestions for treatment.

The employee should be pointed towards other support and resources for menopause issues, such as: HR, Occupational Health, internal leaflets and communications.

4 Clear Boundaries

If the female colleague has instigated the conversation, ask her for an indication of what she wants to talk about before the meeting. If the manager has instigated the meeting outside of the usual pattern of performance meetings, they should state clearly at the beginning what will be discussed.

Prior to the meeting, the manager needs to familiarise themself with existing internal policies and procedures. If they know that they are going to be talking about the impact on the employee of menopause symptoms, they need to be clear on the official policy on reasonable adjustments, such as: flexible working hours, dress code, reallocating duties, or working from home.

If the manager has instigated the meeting to deal with a performance issue, the evidence should be made available to the employee. This may include performance statistics, agreed personal and team goals, absence leave records, time-keeping information or health reports.

The manager should be clear before the start of the meeting what they want to achieve. What would be a good outcome?

5 Communication

Communication includes both listening and asking questions to elicit information.

Asking open questions will enable the employee to talk freely and share their feelings. These are the sorts of questions that start with who, what, where, why when or how. For example:

'What do you feel is affecting your performance?'

'What adjustments to your workspace do you feel would help you?'

Closed questions are useful for confirming information or drawing out facts. They only require a yes or no answer or a factual statement. For example:

'Have you consulted your doctor?'

'How long have you been experiencing these symptoms?'

'What action have you taken?'

Active listening is about hearing what the other person is really saying. This is much more than just waiting for your turn to speak. It is about giving full attention to what is being said and confirming that you have understood the content. The three stages of active listening are:

1. Comprehending – this about understanding what the speaker is saying through their verbal and non-verbal communication. This may require confirmation through questioning.

2. Retaining – remembering what the speaker says is essential to your understanding and how successfully you respond. Retention is lost when you make little effort to listen to the speaker's message or do some other activity while the speaker is talking.

3. Responding – the speaker looks for both your verbal response and your non-verbal response such as body language and facial expressions.

Becoming an active listener takes concentration, determination and practice. It takes self-awareness because you need to notice where your thoughts are going and what you are saying with your body language. But being an active listener leads to better communication and better outcomes.

It is helpful to reflect back parts of the conversation to confirm understanding and to let the employee know that she has been heard. Using the same words that the employee used can be very helpful. This is known as 'Clean Communication'. See an example in Appendix 3.

6 A Good Outcome

There are several measures of a good outcome from this type of conversation. Firstly, that the employee feels heard and understood. She knows what actions are going to be taken.

From the manager's perspective, a good outcome would be achieved when all of the topics have been discussed that led the meeting being requested and there is a plan for resolving the issues. The plan should be specific about who is going to do what and by when which is agreed by both parties.

7 Statements and Questions to Avoid

There are some statements that may obstruct a helpful conversation such as:

'I think it's your menopause'

'My mother/sister/wife had that symptom and she....'

'Have you tried...'

'Aren't you too young/old for menopause?'

'It'll be over soon won't it?'

'Menopause is just natural. It can't be that bad.'

'Well, I went through menopause and it was no problem.'

For Book Bonuses http://www.patduckworth.com/menopausemindthegap

Chapter 5

Reasonable Adjustments

Employers have a legal duty under the Equality Act 2010 to implement reasonable adjustments in the workplace. Under the legislation, employers must make reasonable adjustments where disabled staff would otherwise be put at a substantial disadvantage compared with non-disabled colleagues.

Employers cannot legally justify a failure to comply with a duty to make a reasonable adjustment. This extends to the employer's duty of care for their mental health.

Paragraph 6.33 of the Equality Act 2010 Statutory Code of Practice lists the following possible adjustments, giving an example for each.

- making adjustments to premises
- allocating some of the worker's duties to another person
- transferring the worker to fill an existing vacancy
- altering the worker's hours of working or training

- assigning the worker to a different place of work or training or allowing home working
- allowing the worker to be absent during working or training hours for rehabilitation, assessment or treatment
- allowing the worker to take a period of disability leave
- giving, or arranging for, training or mentoring (whether for the disabled worker or any other person)
- acquiring or modifying equipment
- modifying disciplinary or grievance procedures
- modifying performance-related pay arrangements
- adjusting redundancy selection criteria

The Employment Code para 6.28, lists factors which a tribunal may take into account when deciding whether an adjustment would have been reasonable:

- whether taking any particular step would be effective in preventing the substantial disadvantage
- the practicability of the step
- the financial and other costs of making the adjustment and the extent of any disruption caused
- the extent of the employer's financial or other resources
- the availability to the employer of financial or other assistance to help make an adjustment, e.g. advice from Access to Work
- the type and size of the employer.

Here are some suggestions for reasonable adjustments for employees experiencing menopause symptoms that have been drawn from recent research:

- Access to cold drinking water. This will enable women to stay hydrated which will assist with hot flushes, clearer thinking and concentration.

- Personal storage space for sanitary items and medication. Some women experience heavier and more frequent periods during peri-menopause. It is important to provide discreet storage in open plan offices, particularly where there is a hot desking policy, to avoid embarrassment.

- Flexible working times to combat issues caused by sleep disturbance. Later start times can be a very acceptable solution.

- Review ventilation around workstations. Women experiencing hot flushes may need to sit closer to a window, air conditioning unit or a fan.

- Evaluate uniforms for women employees and consider whether any adjustments or an alternative uniform for women is required. Uniforms that are close-fitted or made of man-made fibres can exacerbate hot flushes, causing women to sweat profusely.

- Easy access to toilet facilities, including when women employees are traveling or working in temporary locations.

- A rest room for women whose duties require constant standing or prolonged sitting

For more information on reasonable adjustments see Appendix 4

For Book Bonuses http://www.patduckworth.com/menopausemindthegap

Chapter 6

A Strategic Approach to Managing Menopause

A strategic approach to supporting employees at menopause in the workplace is still a rarity but is becoming more recognised as important to employee wellbeing and optimal performance, particularly in the public sector. It supports a culture of inclusivity, diversity and equality and improves morale.

A 2019 poll in "Employee Benefits" found that more than three-quarters (77%) of respondents did not have a strategy in place at their organisations to address the menopause, or to support female staff who may be experiencing menopausal symptoms. The poll also found that 15% had implemented flexible working in order to help staff who are experiencing the menopause, while 9% had introduced workplace adjustments, such as access to cool air.

No respondents to the poll had considered line manager training on menopausal symptoms and workplace adjustments or implementing leave policies that extend beyond traditional sick leave. A strategic approach to menopause illustrates an organisation's commitment to employee wellbeing and can form part of their defence in related cases brought under employment law.

There are a number of elements that can be included in such a strategy including communication, training, a menopause policy and specific roles within the organisation. The extent that organisations decide to commit to these elements will depend on their values as well as their size and demographic structure of the employees.

1 Employee Survey

An employee survey is an effective tool to gauge the current level of understanding of menopause issues, satisfaction with existing policies and interest in the development of specific menopause policies.

Following the implementation of further communication, training, and other actions, surveys can measure engagement or effectiveness of the implementation of the plan.

2 Communication

Creating a communication plan is an early stage in a strategic approach to managing menopause. It raises awareness of the issues for women, their colleagues and managers and signals that this is an open subject for discussion within the organisation.

Communication can be educational about menopause and point employees to resources and policies.

The plan may include hardcopy materials such as: leaflets, fact sheets, FAQs, brochures, and leadership packs. In larger organisations with an

Intranet, the plan may include dedicated pages with awareness and educational material.

Once the menopause strategy has been implemented, communications may include details of training and workshops, celebrations of events that have taken place and updates.

3 Training

Training on menopause issues can be both educational and raise awareness. It may take place in person or online depending on the circumstances of the organisation.

The content of the training should be tailored to the needs of the audience:

- Employees at menopause – symptoms, how to recognise them, common triggers, options for managing symptoms, advocating for support, and where support is available.
- HR and Occupational Health Professionals – understanding of menopause and potential effect on performance, employment law, reasonable adjustments, good practice
- Line-Managers – why menopause is a workplace issue, understanding the symptoms and effects, legal requirements, reasonable adjustments and how to have a sensitive conversation.
- Staff – awareness of menopause symptoms and impact at work and providing support to colleagues.

4 Informal Support Groups

Informal groups enable employees to provide peer-to-peer support. They may take the form of a coffee, lunch or after-work group which can take place in person or online.

These groups work best if there is no agenda, but they can include a speaker or presentation if the attendees request it. They should be open to all and provide a safe and respectful place to discuss menopause issues.

This can be a place where other workplace menopause information is available. There is no expectation of solving employee workplace issues in these sessions.

5 Helpline

Some larger organisations have set up menopause helplines to provide employees with a ready source of information and support. It may be organised by HR, Occupational Health or Equality and Diversity.

Such helplines are most effective if contact is anonymous so that callers are free to discuss personal issues.

6 Menopause Champion

It is rewarding to see more organisations creating and implementing menopause policies. Some organisations are going a step further and appointing Menopause Champions. But what is the role of a Menopause Champion and how can they add value to employers and organisations?

The British Menopause Society suggests that organisations should create: "Both formal and informal sources of support should be created and detailed in guidance. To whom and to where women, or line managers, can go when they need some additional help and advice. This could be a named person in HR or just the occupational health team. It will be different for each organisation. You may even have a named 'Menopause Champion'. Whoever it is, it should be clear in the guidance who and how they can be contacted."

The role of the Menopause Champion is voluntary and they do not need to be a member of HR or Occupational Health. The most important characteristics of a champion is that they are enthusiastic about helping women at this stage, they have knowledge of menopause, and they are comfortable talking about it.

The tasks they undertake will vary from organisation to organisation but could include:

- Raising awareness of menopause and the support that the organisation offers
- Arranging workshops for employees and managers
- Creating a support network
- Directing women colleagues to support and advice
- Liaising with senior management on providing appropriate support
- Being part of the working group or project group to create and implement a Menopause Policy
- Acting as a liaison for suggestions from women colleagues on reasonable adjustments
- Keeping up to date with menopause issues.

The Menopause Champion is not there to provide treatment advice or resolve performance issues.

The role can be an interesting development opportunity for a woman who is interested in expanding her network of influence and contributing to corporate objectives.

Depending on the size of the organisation, more than one Menopause Champion may be needed.

7 Menopause Sponsor

Larger organisations with multiple sites and management committees may consider appointing a Menopause Sponsor. A suitable person for this role would be employed at a senior management level with access to the executives and management team.

The role of the Sponsor is to liaise between the employees who are implementing the menopause policies and the executives and organisation's committees. They would be expected to raise menopause issues at organisational level and ensure that these issues are considered when organisational policies are being created and implemented.

The Sponsor would be part of the Menopause Policy Team and report on progress to senior managers.

8 Menopause Policy

Specific policies relating to menopause can be included in existing employment policies. Bringing policies together in one policy signals the organisation's commitment to supporting colleagues at this stage of life. It will enable employees to speak openly about the subject

Best practice in creating a menopause policy is to carry out a confidential staff survey to find out what employees are experiencing and what support they require. It will also help to gauge support for the implementation of a policy. It may be surprising that this is like pushing at an open door.

There are a number of elements that can be included in a Menopause Policy such as:

- Statement of organisational values
- Aims
- Scope
- Glossary of terms
- Support that is or will be available:
  - Training
  - Awareness and communication
  - Responsibilities: individuals, line-managers, managers, employer, HR, Occupational Health, Trade Unions and any other parties

- ♦ Reasonable Adjustments
- ♦ Other sources of information
- ♦ Contact points
- FAQs
- Basic menopause information

If an Employment Tribunal Case arises involving issues relating to an employee at menopause, being able to produce a Menopause Policy will be one very powerful piece of evidence. Employers will also need to demonstrate how it has been implemented.

For Book Bonuses http://www.patduckworth.com/menopausemindthegap

Chapter 7

Retaining and Developing Senior Women
– Jill McCulloch

C onsidered to be the upper end of the 'prime working age' group of 25 – 55y, women over 50 are seen as, 'passing the peak of their career and approaching retirement.' (1) Sadly, many women leave full-time work during their menopause and the workforce loses a resource of wisdom and experience built up over decades.

We have heard in previous chapters the symptoms which undermine menopausal women's desire to remain in their position: the sleeplessness leading to exhaustion, the brain fog causing intermittent confusion, the anxiety and loss of confidence, the embarrassment of acute physical symptoms and the stigma of being "past it" to name but a few.

Macro level change

In order for cultural change to occur, complete transparency is required, active openness and public debate.

Former Arthur Rank Hospice chief executive Dr Lynn Morgan MBE shares, "In the current workplace people are happy to be identified as a multitude of different gender mixes, people have affairs, leave their partners, admit to a hangover in the office etc but the last taboo is having a period and even worse having one that you cannot control.

Then of course the hormones really get going and women may have hot flushes, tears, anxiety, depression and female members of my teams over the years have said 'I just don't feel like me anymore.'"

Look at the change in public consciousness around mental illness for example, where the public outpouring and debate has impacted work practices and thankfully even legislation. As the World Health Organisation points out: 'One in four people in the world will be affected by mental or neurological disorders at some point in their lives. Around 450 million people currently suffer from such conditions, placing mental disorders among the leading causes of ill-health and disability worldwide.' [2] And yet, 50% of the population go through "the change" with sometimes traumatic physical and emotional changes with a significant proportion of those with mental illnesses being triggered by a dramatic hormonal shift.

So, who can lead the debate and how?

Radio DJ and TV presenter Jo Whiley opened up to Woman and Home about their menopause experiences. Women's magazines often tackle female issues valiantly that never see the light of day in the mainstream press. The Equality Act in August 2020 brought protection but according to the Henpicked website [3], the Act is not necessarily being followed in the workplace.

Individual Change

"I just don't feel like me anymore", is exactly how so many women feel undergoing menopause. Anxious, wobbly for no reason, unable to get a full night's sleep, women lose command of their emotional responses, I've seen powerful, confident women collapse in tears over dropping a pan of peas.

First and foremost, you want your senior people to accept the reality of the situation and preferably switch to a positive perspective. That doesn't mean discounting hormone replacement therapy, (HRT), that can deal with the symptoms, but you want them to positively embrace this new phase in their life, often described as "Wise Woman". If you are to retain all this experience and understanding in the organisation then you want to shift their role to suit their new set of beliefs.

Many of us, not only menopausal women, seek meaning and purpose at this time of life. We are questioning our role in the world and the impact we have on it. Investing in coaching allows them to recognise the person they are now. A female leader may be substantially different to the woman she was at the beginning of her career. This allows her to step into this new stage in life positively and powerfully, exploring her values, empowering her personal brand and tackling new self-limiting beliefs.

For many women, this time coincides with fewer financial obligations and the arrival of grandchildren. Having lost confidence, they know they will be "useful" providing childcare to grandchildren. Sometimes the first time the manager hears about the struggle with menopause is when she hands in her notice! Rather than lose those skills altogether, if possible, offer part-time working.

Senior level job shares can be tremendously successful, especially where each provides flexibility and emotional support for the other. They can also provide opportunities for succession planning and mentoring on the job. Indeed, mentoring is a powerful way to give back by sharing wisdom and experience and enable colleagues to build relationships across diverse sectors of the organisation.

An additional challenge of menopause is that the impact can be different for each person, particularly when it comes to the mind. The neuroscience around hormonal impact on the emotional elements of the brain is ongoing. It would be fair to conclude that the hormones flood the pre-existing neural pathways that lead to negative thinking – igniting the person's unique mix of saboteurs or self-limiting beliefs. Negative neural pathways can be dramatically reduced and even eliminated through consistent disruption.

For years I encouraged people to first notice and recognise when they are triggered and give the saboteur a name. Then get up and move, disrupt the neural pathway with the following, where possible and of course these are not simple in the middle of the office! For example:

1. Walk quickly – It forces oxygen through the brain and triggers feel good hormones.
2. Go outside – Get some fresh air because a change of environment can trigger change of mood.
3. Run up and down the stairs – Again, it oxygenates the brain and triggers feel good hormones
4. Dance like a mad thing – Oxygenates, makes you laugh and it's a great mood switch but tricky in an open plan office
5. Sing – It fills the lungs and triggers feel good hormones

One powerful coaching tool that I use with my clients helps to build mental fitness [4]. Mental fitness is the capacity to handle life's challenges with a positive mindset instead of getting stressed, upset or any other negative emotion. It is possible to gain this control at any point in your life and then, once faced with triggers caused by hormonal imbalance in menopause, you have the tools and skills to manage the transition with more ease. Naturally this is a relief for each individual band also the people around us.

I am currently in the menopause and still have the potential to become dramatically triggered, particularly by technology. Now, though, I have the ability to let go of the negative thoughts and re-engage my 'Sage brain', allowing me to make decisions based upon discernment rather than reacting with negative emotions.

Senior Women want to remain in command in the boardroom, in meetings and with their team. Mental Fitness supports them in doing this, now and when they reach menopause. So, let's open up and support our senior women to take a positive viewpoint of the menopause as a time to reflect more, share, mentor and empower more – if that is what 'Wise Woman' means to them.

Most of all, let's just listen with empathy to those of us in any way demoralised by the change.

Jill McCulloch

Jill McCulloch is a Leadership and Business Coach, coaching her clients to maximise their potential. www.coachyou.co.uk

References

1. Organisation for Economic Co-operation and Development
2. Mental disorders affect one in four people – WHO www.who.in-t›whr›media_centre›press_release Geneva, 4 October 2020
3. 'Does menopause in the workplace support or threaten equality?' 2018, https://menopauseintheworkplace.co.uk/equality/menopause-work-place-equality/
4. Mental Fitness - www.positiveintelligence.com

For Book Bonuses http://www.patduckworth.com/menopausemindthegap

Chapter 8

How to Avoid Legal Procedures Legislation

Although there is no specific legislation relating to menopause in the workplace, there is legislation to protect employees experiencing symptoms at this stage of life. This includes:

1. Health and Safety at Work Act 1974 and The Management of Health and Safety at Work Regulations 1999

The Act requires employers to ensure the health, safety and welfare of all workers. The Regulations require employers to assess the risks of ill health (including stress related conditions) arising from work-related activities, ensuring that the hazards are removed or proper control measures are put in place to reduce the risk so far as is reasonably practical.

2. The Equality Act 2010 forbids discrimination against people because of various protected characteristics. People at menopause are largely covered under four protected characteristics: sex, age, gender reassignment, and disability. It is also concerned with the removal of unnecessary barriers to the full participation of disabled people in work and society.

Under the Equality Act, a disabled person is defined as someone who has a mental or physical impairment that has a substantial and long-term adverse effect on the person's ability to carry out normal day-to-day activities.

Employers have a duty to make reasonable adjustments for disabled workers, where failure to do so would place the disabled worker at a substantial disadvantage compared to non-disabled workers. They must not treat employees less favourably than others as a result of a disability.

Part 1(1) of the Act specifically places a duty on Public Sector employers:

"An authority to which this section applies must, when making decisions of a strategic nature about how to exercise its functions, have due regard to the desirability of exercising them in a way that is designed to reduce the inequalities of outcome which result from socio-economic disadvantage."

Sections of the Act that may relate to employment cases involving people at menopause:

Sec 20 Adjustments for disabled persons

Sec 26 Harassment

Sec 29 – 60 Employment etc

Sec 61 – 63 Occupational Pension Schemes

Sec 64 - 80 Equality of Terms

Sec 113 - 148 Enforcement

Sec 149 Public Sector Equality Duty

Para 6.33 Equality Act 2010 Statutory Code of Practice Employment etc – Reasonable Adjustments

This is not a comprehensive list and other sections of the Act may apply.

Costs

Employment Tribunal cases are costly in terms of the time and preparation that needs to be put into them by the organisation and their legal representatives. If the judgement goes in favour of the employee there are the additional costs of compensation.

There is the reputational cost and damage to your brand of being seen as a bad employer of women.

Employment Tribunal cases can also have a depressive effect on the morale of other employees

Recent Case Law

As of November 2020, three cases relating to menopause have been decided by the Employment Tribunal.

Merchant v British Telecoms Plc 2012

In this case, the employee, Ms Merchant, alleged that she had been discriminated against on the grounds of her gender when her employer failed to deal with her menopause symptoms in the same way it would have dealt with other medical conditions.

Ms Merchant had been subject to underperformance procedures for a few years, culminating in a final warning. The performance issues persisted so a further performance process was commenced. During a meeting to discuss the performance issues, Ms Merchant provided her manager with a letter from her doctor explaining that she was going through the menopause and that this was affecting her ability to concentrate. She also referred to her menopause on several occasions during the meeting.

The manager chose not to carry out any further investigation of her medical condition, in breach of the company's performance management policy. Instead, he made a judgment on Ms Merchant's health and the impact on her ability to carry out her role by comparing it to what he knew of the menopause experiences of his wife and HR adviser, despite all women experiencing the menopause differently.

The Tribunal upheld Ms Merchant's claims and pointed out that the manager would never have adopted "this bizarre and irrational approach" with other non-female-related conditions. This was in contravention of The Equality Act 2010 which sets out that sex discrimination occurs where, because of sex, A (in this case the employer) treats B (the employee) less favourably than they treat or would treat others.

Davies v Scottish Courts and Tribunals Service (2018)

Ms Davies suffered from heavy bleeding, severe anaemia, memory loss and a "fuzzy" feeling related to her menopause. Her employer recognised her disability and made reasonable adjustments for her.

In February 2017, Ms Davies began taking a medication which needed to be dissolved in water. On the day in question, she was working in court and, upon returning from the lavatory, was concerned to note that her jug of water was being drunk by two members of the public. She could not remember whether she had dissolved her medication in the water and so informed the two men that her medication had been dissolved in it.

Despite her condition making her flustered and forgetful, and her 20 years of unblemished service, Ms Davies was subsequently dismissed for gross misconduct on the grounds that she had knowingly misled the two men and management. It was stated that she should have known the water would turn pink once the medication was in it. She was accused of bringing the court into disrepute.

In addition to being unfairly dismissed, the tribunal held that there was a clear link between Ms Davies' dismissal and her conduct and that her conduct was affected by her disability.

Ms Davies was reinstated and awarded £19,000. £14,000 of which was back pay and £5,000 due to injury of feelings.

A v Bon Marché Ltd (2019)

The claimant, A, was a senior supervisor at the retailer, and had worked there for 37 years. She was one of the top sellers for the company.

In 2017 her manager started ridiculing her as she was going through menopause. He called her a dinosaur in front of customers and encouraged other staff to laugh at his comments.

During a company restructure in 2018, A had to apply for her own post and was the only applicant. Shortly after she discovered that her manager had encouraged other staff to apply for her role.

A tried to raise her menopause issues with her manager and higher management but no action was taken. She suffered some significant sickness absence but managed to return to her role on a phased basis working short-

71

er hours. However, A's manager placed her on a full shift for the following week. She resigned and suffered a complete breakdown due to the harassment and bullying she had endured.

A claimed that her treatment by her manager amounted to harassment and or direct discrimination on grounds of age and sex. The definition of direct discrimination is contained in section 13 of the Equality Act 2010.

"A person (A) discriminates against another (B) if, because of a protected characteristic, A treats B less favourably than A treats or would treat others.

The definition of harassment is contained in section 26 of the Equality Act 2010.

"A person (A) harasses another (B) if:

(a) A engages in unwanted conduct related to a relevant protected characteristic, and

(b) the conduct has the purpose or effect of

(i) violating B's dignity, or

(ii) creating an intimidating, hostile, degrading, humiliating or offensive environment for B."

A was successful on both counts and was awarded £10,000 for loss of earnings, and £18,000 for injury to feelings as a result of the serious bullying and harassment she had suffered.

The Lessons

- Failure to take account of an employee's experience of menopause symptoms may be seen as contravention of The Equality Act 2010.
- Although menopause is not an illness, if the symptoms are frequent, intense and go on over a sustained period, they can be classed as a disability under the Equality Act 2010.

- Harassment by managers based on an employee's age and gender falls under the definition of direct discrimination in Sec 13 and harassment in Sec 26 of the Equality Act 2010. Comments about a person's menopause may be judged to fall under these sections and are therefore unlawful.

- If an employee reports that their performance at work is being affected by menopause symptoms, management must be able to show that they took account of the issue and took steps to comply with employment and equality legislation.

For Book Bonuses http://www.patduckworth.com/menopausemindthegap

Case Study
The Effect of Menopause Symptoms (Part 2)

Previously - After over eighteen months of feeling unwell, Sam has walked into your office and told you that she is thinking of resigning.

You say to Sam that you really want to chat this through with her before she makes a final decision. Sam agrees and you arrange a time and a place for a private chat.

Fortunately, during the last 12 months your organisation has been working towards implementing a menopause policy. A steering committee has been consulting with women colleagues, information leaflets have been produced and managers and some staff have already been on training sessions. You feel that if menopause is the underlying issue behind Sam's decision then you know how to talk about it.

When you have the meeting with Sam you remind her what a valued member of staff she is and how you would be very sorry to lose her. You ask her about the reasons behind her current thinking about leaving.

Sam tells you that she still loves her job, but she has been feeling below her best for some time now. She has spoken to the doctor on several occasions but doesn't feel that she is getting to the root of the problem. She thinks it may be hormonal as she's in her late 40s and she feels a bit embarrassed talking about it.

Sam says that it has helped that there is now a women's group in the office who are making it easier to talk about these issues. They've had a session talking about menopause and she thinks

Menopause: Mind the Gap

this may be part of the problem. She is going to raise this with her doctor.

You reassure Sam that there are adjustments that can be made to support her and ask her what she would find most helpful, including an appointment with the Occupational Health Nurse.

Sam says that she feels relieved just to talk about it. The extra stress of trying to conceal how she has felt has added to the problem at work and at home.

You discuss next steps and agree a date to review how things are working out.

Following her discussion with the Occupational Health Nurse, Sam moves to a later start time and reduces her working hours by five hours a week. A workstation assessment is carried out and a few minor changes made.

By the time of the review Sam is looking more energised and reports feeling less stressed and much happier. Her performance has improved and she is taking on new tasks. A lot of her previous enthusiasm for the job has returned.

Sam volunteers to be part of the Menopause Steering Committee.

If you need help with raising awareness of menopause issues through communication, training or workshops see www.patduckworth.com or contact me directly pat@patduckworth.com

Case Study 1
My Experience of Early Menopause

24 February 2012 – my 36th Birthday! My husband and I had the day off and we arranged to go for a pub lunch while our boy was at nursery. But first I had a hospital appointment to get some test results. My 36th Birthday became the day I was officially diagnosed with early menopause – the day I became an 'old woman'!

My day didn't turn out as I had planned, instead my head was in a spin. Although having a diagnosis explained a lot, why I had been feeling so awful and tired all the time, I had to deal with the fact I wasn't going to have any more children. It made me grateful for having my son, and that we hadn't left it any longer to start a family. We hadn't ever planned to have a large family, in fact there hadn't been much planning about having a family at all, we just knew we would at some point. But now that choice had been taken away.

Although my diagnosis was confirmed on my birthday, I had had my suspicions that I was going through early menopause but had dismissed it. I had gone to my GP with irregular and very heavy periods which was really unusual for me. Since having my son they had changed dramatically. However, it was the sleepless nights, the hot sweats, weight gain, and irritability that I was experiencing that made me realise there was something wrong. I worried that it might be something worse. So, after several rounds of blood tests and being referred to a consultant it was a slight relief to know it was the menopause.

The following day I was back at work and my colleagues asked how my birthday had been. I don't think they expected the answer I gave them. I decided to be open with them and tell them about my diagnosis as we work in a small office and I knew my irritability and mood swings would not have gone unnoticed. Being women, they understood but even though I was the youngest in the team the others hadn't yet experienced any symptoms of the menopause so they didn't fully understand the side effects that I was suffering.

Fortunately for me, I have a very good friend, Maggie, who is a Personal Trainer. One day I called her in tears having realised that this wasn't going to go away and I needed to deal with it. I didn't want to be old before my time. It was affecting me physically and mentally and I thought Maggie would be able to at least deal with the physical element.

Maggie was brilliant, listening to me sob as I told her what the doctors had said. She set me a tailored programme to get me eating the right things and a routine of exercises to help me lose weight. What she did for me was more than losing weight, it was about me regaining control and my confidence.

My consultant advised going on HRT (hormone replacement therapy) due to my age and because I had a young son to look after. One of the side effects of early menopause is osteoporosis (something my mum suffers from) so, although HRT gets some bad press, I did my research and decided it was the best thing for me to do. It took a while and a couple of different consultants to get the right HRT and dose but it has made a massive difference. I felt more like me again and the side effects disappeared.

One side effect that I found hard to deal with or shake was my ability to perform at work. I had found work a struggle ever since I came back from maternity leave and I put it down to 'baby brain.' I wasn't focused, easily losing concentration and was really forgetful. I felt like giving it all up and spoke to Jane, my boss, but she was keen to keep me.

Once I started training with Maggie I turned a corner. My HRT was taking care of my symptoms. I was sleeping better, my weight was dropping, my mood lightened and I was less irritable. Jane saw the progress I was making and decided to give me more responsibility and I came on board as a shareholder in the agency. That gave me the push I needed to realise that I was in charge of me and just because I was going through an early menopause did not make me an old woman, far from it.

I embarked on several physical challenges I would never even have dreamt of doing in my twenties: obstacle races and half marathons. I also qualified to teach kettlebell alongside Maggie as a hobby. All of this helped me regain my self-confidence and helped with my working life too.

Now I work out most mornings or have time to myself when the house is quiet to be able to clear my head. If this isn't possible, I take the dog for a walk at lunchtime to force myself to take a lunch break from work. The physical aspect of my training helps with my mental state.

I still get brain fog regularly and I am hopelessly forgetful, but I have put processes in place to help me deal with my work on a day to day basis. I use an online calendar that has notifications set for appointments and I add reminders too, to pay car tax, book an optician appointment etc. I write a to do list every morning, not to make myself feel bad when I get to the end of the day and I haven't completed it, but so I don't forget. Writing these lists has helped me be more productive and stay focussed.

I have also set up better working practises such as checking emails at certain points through the day rather than acting on each email as it arrives. Also, my work is flexible. We have agreed that if I have a nightmare morning and get to work late, it doesn't matter, as long as I still get my work done.

I have lost weight, I sleep better, I am less irritable, I have got my confidence back and I am a happier me. Some days are harder than others but that's fine as some days I am more productive. I try to learn from each day and what I can do to improve on the next. Self-belief is a great power but you need the support around you to make that happen. I feel very lucky to have that support at work from Jane, and in my personal life from Maggie.

Lesley Fettes

Lesley Fettes is a Director at Network Design,

Case Study 2
Implementing a Menopause Policy in Cheshire Fire and Rescue Service

Background

Equality, diversity and inclusion sits at the heart of everything Cheshire Fire Service (CFS) does and underpins its approach to delivering an excellent emergency service as an employer.

The Authority believe in and defines equality in its widest sense, enabling all of its people to be themselves and removing barriers to services, creating opportunities and safer communities.

Committed to Equality – CFS ensures fair and equitable access to all of its services, wherever they are needed

Committed to Diversity – CFS recognises and embraces difference within its workforce and among those who live, work and travel through the county.

Committed to Inclusion – CFS welcome and celebrate diversity within the community and aim to be an employer of choice, creating an environment where everyone can develop their talents, prosper and succeed.

Cheshire Fire Service is committed to recruiting, developing, supporting and retaining a workforce which better reflects the diversity of the communities it services and the wider population. Furthermore, a diverse workforce with an open culture has been shown to be more productive, by enabling people to be themselves while at work and bringing new ideas and innovation to the table. It is also committed to engaging and supporting its people

Raising Awareness

The first step was the formation of a working group which was made up of individuals from a cross-section of the Service working different work patterns, in different departments, and delivering different functions. Some of the working group had undergone the menopause or were perimenopausal and were able to offer contributions based on their own experiences.

I attended a conference in recognising and supporting menopause in the workplace and also researched the subject. From that I identified the symptoms and challenges that can present, and as a group we identified how these symptoms could affect different roles and the reasonable adjustments that could be applied to support our staff.

The Limitless Network Chair also communicated the intentions to the email distribution list which includes all female staff (operational and non-operational), inviting feedback and responses.

Mental Health Awareness day was highlighted and supported by the Service in October 2019. This resulted in a vast number of activities to support mental health and wellbeing being arranged service wide and one event was planned and implemented specifically around the subject of menopause and the impact it can have in terms of mental ill health.

The CFS menopause policy was written and officially launched at the annual International Women's Day conference in 2020. The event included the official launch, training and coping strategies provided by Women's Health Strategist Pat Duckworth. There was a discussion about menopause from a husband's perspective lead by one of our firefighter's whose wife had been through a difficult experience.

Additional awareness raising will be done by further training to everyone in the organisation from entry level to senior managers irrespective of gender.

All events were supported by the Chief Fire Officer, Mark Cashin, who champions and promotes equality, diversity and inclusion priorities.

World Menopause Day was highlighted through the dissemination and promotion of literature produced by Fire Brigade Union. It was instructed for the literature to be displayed in prominent locations to encourage open dialogue around the subject.

Training

CFS are planning for training to be delivered in groups to everyone in the organisation, irrespective of gender or role.

Some of this training will be delivered by the EDI officer, but the training delivered to our female staff will be delivered by a Subject Matter Expert. We feel it important to have someone who has walked the walk and who can relate on a personal level.

Additionally, an eLearning package will be introduced to reinforce and support the training and knowledge acquisition and it will be refreshed on a bi-annual frequency. This training will be mandatory for all staff.

The subject of menopause will also be included in the broad equality training delivered by the EDI officer to our new starters in the service.

The menopause policy sits within the suite of policies easily accessible to all staff.

Reasonable Adjustments

- Reasonable adjustments have been made in the workplace for colleagues who have requested them. These include:

- Provision of extra uniform

- Provision of uniform which adapts to accommodate bloating

- Use of quiet rooms where possible

- Flexible working

- Use of hand fans, desk fans or seating near an open window

- Any other reasonable adjustments as per the Occupational Health and/or GP recommendations

- Specific requests during recruitment and promotions will be considered on a case by case basis, to take into account the needs of the individual.

- Sanitary packs have been made available in all vehicles and fire appliances.

The above list is not exhaustive. Other reasonable adjustments will be considered on a case by case basis in conjunction with Occupational Health and/or HR.

Creating and Implementing a Menopause Policy

CFS has adopted a collaborative approach including the Women's Network, EDI officer, Occupational Health and HR.

The process of creating our Menopause Policy involved:

- Establish a working group

- Carry out research

- Staff engagement

- Senior Management team sign off

- Trade Union sign off

Now that the policy has been launched, the next steps are the training and embedding of it.

Menopause related issues can be supported and addressed through the quarterly Limitless network meetings or through the social activities that are arranged through the network.

In addition, the network is currently developing sub support groups made up by champions such as menopause and maternity.

We have had a very positive response from our female colleagues. The 'Each for Equal' conference, where the policy was officially launched and initial training delivered, received overwhelmingly positive feedback.

Our future plans to further implement and embed the Menopause Policy include:

- The delivery of initial and refresher training

- Development of menopause champions and a menopause support network

- Continued discussions around menopause to eliminate taboo

- Source menopause literature/ handbooks and issue to all departments and workplaces.

- Monitor the embedding of the policy and make adjustments if required

My advice to other organisations to other organisations would be:

1. Take advantage of the formalities of a policy instead of guidance notes to set out the expectations required of all, from the individual experiencing the symptoms to the managers of the individual.

2. The policy will enable you to have a central location for all useful links and information to enable the individual to learn and prepare themselves instead of burying their head in the sand.

It is too early to tell what the effect of the Policy will be since the policy was introduced in March and business as usual has been affected by the COVID-19 virus. I believe that this policy will provide invaluable support to managers, colleagues, and the affected individuals.

Hannah Caulfield 2020

Hannah Caulfield is a Watch Manager at Cheshire Fire Service and the Chair of the CFS Limitless Network.

References

A v Bon Marche 2019 https://assets.publishing.service.gov.uk/media/5e21 b7a1e5274a6c3f52a4e1/A_v_Bonmarche__in_Administration _-4107766.19-Final.pdf

Advisory, Conciliation and Arbitration Service (ACAS), Menopause at work, https://www.acas.org.uk/index.aspx?articleid=6752

Australian Financial Review (2020) 'The elephant in the room for executive women', https://www.afr.com/work-and-careers/management/the-elephant-in-the-room-for-executive-women-20200114-p53rd1

Brewis, J. 'Menopause and the Workplace' 2019 https://www.youtube.com/watch?v=WR1U6TEqqR4 Open University

Brewis, J., et al 'The effects of menopause transition on women's economic participation in the UK' 2016, DoE https://www.gov.uk/government/publications/menopause-transition-effects-on-womens-economic-participation

Brewis, J. 'Menopause at work: what does the evidence say?', 2020, https://menopauseintheworkplace.co.uk/menopause-at-work/menopause-at-work-what-does-the-evidence-say/

Davies v Scottish Courts and Tribunals Service (2018) https://assets.publishing.service.gov.uk/media/5afc31a8ed915d0de80ffd2c/Ms_M_Davies_v_Scottish_Courts_and_Tribunals_Service_4104575_2017_Final.pdf

Employee Benefits (2019) https://employeebenefits.co.uk/poll-77-strategy-menopause/

Employment: Statutory Code of Practice. (The EHRC Employment Code) https://www.equalityhumanrights.com/en/publication-download/employment-statutory-code-practice

Equality Act 2010, Guidance. Guidance on matters to be taken into account in determining questions relating to the definition of disability. (2011) https://assets.publishing.service.gov.uk/government/uploads/system/uploads/attachment_data/file/570382/Equality_Act_2010-disability_definition.pdf

Fineberg, N., Haddad, P., Carpenter, L., Gannon, B., Sharpe, R., Young, A., Joyce, E., Rowe, J., Wellsted, D., Nutt, D. and Sahakian, B. (2013). *The size, burden and cost of disorders of the brain in the UK.* Journal of Psychopharmacology, 27(9), pp.761-770.

Griffiths, A., MacLennan, S., Wong, y., *Women's Experience of Working through the Menopause,* 2010, Institute of Work, Health & Organisation

Griffiths, A. et al., *Menopause and Work: An Electronic Survey of Employees' Attitudes in the UK* (2013) https://pubmed.ncbi.nlm.nih.gov/23973049/

Harvard Business Review (2020), *Is menopause a taboo in Your Organization?* https://hbr.org/2020/02/is-menopause-a-taboo-in-your-organization

Holloway, D., '*Not just 'hot flushes' – why it's time employers took the menopause seriously'* Personnel Today, October 2019

HR Review (Feb 2014) *'It Costs Over £30k to Replace a Staff Member'*, https://www.hrreview.co.uk/hr-news/recruitment/it-costs-over-30k-to-re-place-a-staff-member/50677

Hult Ashridge (2019), *Speaking truth to power at work*, https://static1.squarespace.com/static/597729cbcf81e0f87c7f6c61/t/5d09071aff-3d870001a13ce3/1560872755660/Speaking_Truth_to_Power_Re-port_2019_Final+1.pdf

Institute of Work, Health & Organisation, *Women's Experience of Working through the Menopause, A Report for The British Occupational Health Research Foundation* 2010

Merchant v British Telecom plc https://www.thehrdirector.com/legal-up-dates/archive/failure-to-address-menopause-amounted-to-sex-discrimina-tion/

My Menopause Doctor, Menopause and Work – New Guidelines (2018) https://www.menopausedoctor.co.uk/menopause/menopause-work-new-guidelines

North American Menopause Society (NAMS), 2020, *New Study Links Number of Menopause Symptoms With Job Performance*, https://www.menopause.org/docs/default-source/press-release/menopause-symp-toms-and-work-performance-11-30-20.pdf

NHS *Overview of Hysterectomy* https://www.nhs.uk/conditions/hysterecto-my/

Re:Jerusalem, *Women's Health Care Market Growth,* (2020), https://rejeru-salem.com/280306/17-8-billion-worth-womens-health-care-market-led-by-bayer-ag-allergan-merck-co-pfizer-inc-and-more/

Stewart, M., (2019) *What Women Want at Menopause*

Trades Union Congress, *Supporting working Women through the meno-pause: Guidance for Union representatives* (2013) https://www.tuc.org.uk/resource/supporting-women-through-menopause

Unison: *Proving Disability and Reasonable Adjustments: A Guide to evidence under the Equality Act 2010* September 2018 https://www.unison.org.uk/content/uploads/2018/10/Proving-Disability-and-Reasonable-Adjust-ments-Oct2018.pdf

Unison. *Menopause: The menopause is a workplace issue: Guidance and model policy 2019* https://www.unison.org.uk/content/uploads/2019/10/25831.pdf

Wales TUC (2017) *The Menopause in the Workplace: A toolkit for trade union-ists, https://www.tuc.org.uk/sites/default/files/Menopause%20toolkit%20Eng%20FINAL.pdf*

Resources

Appendix 1 Definitions

Various terms are used in connection with menopause. It is useful to understand what is generally meant by these terms, particularly in conversations with colleagues and health professionals

Climacteric – the ongoing changes and symptoms that occur during the transition period when ovarian and hormonal production decline. This stage may last 15-20 years between the ages of 40 and 60. It can be compared to the years of puberty and adolescence.

Premature Ovarian Failure (POF) or Primary Ovarian Insufficiency (POI) -menopause that takes place before age 40. It occurs in 1 to 4 per cent of women. It can be precipitated by illnesses and medical interventions including radiotherapy and hysterectomy, but in up to 70 per cent of cases there is no obvious medical reason. Women experiencing early menopause have an increased risk of health issues such as osteoporosis and cardiovascular disease because of the reduced levels of oestrogen.

Pre-menopause – the early years of the transition period when menstrual periods may become irregular and, sometimes, heavier. Other menopause symptoms may be experienced. Generally, this stage starts after the age of 40.

Perimenopause – this is the stage either side of the last menstrual period when most physical changes become noticeable and menstrual periods may change becoming irregular, heavier or lighter.

Menopause – the last menstrual period. Women do not know if this is their last period until they have not had a menstrual bleed for 12 months.

Post-menopause – this relates to the years after the last period up to the end of life. It overlaps with the perimenopause.

Medically Induced Menopause

Hysterectomy

Hysterectomy is the surgical procedure to remove the womb (uterus). About 60,000 hysterectomies are carried out in the UK every year and over 600,000 in the US.

It is commonly carried out to treat conditions such as:

- Heavy periods
- Long-term pelvic pain
- Fibroids (non-cancerous tumours)
- Cancer of the ovaries, uterus, cervix or the fallopian tubes.

This is a major operation and should only be carried out if other treatments have not been successful. It involves up to five days in hospital and six to eight weeks recovery time.

There are four types of hysterectomy:

- total hysterectomy – the womb and cervix (neck of the womb) are removed; this is the most commonly performed operation
- subtotal hysterectomy – the main body of the womb is removed, leaving the cervix in place
- total hysterectomy with bilateral salpingo-oophorectomy – the womb, cervix, fallopian tubes (salpingectomy) and ovaries (oophorectomy) are removed
- radical hysterectomy – the womb and surrounding tissues are removed, including the fallopian tubes, part of the vagina, ovaries, lymph glands and fatty tissue

If the ovaries are left intact there is a chance that the woman will experience menopause within five years of the operation. However, if the ovaries are removed as part of the procedure the woman will go into menopause immediately after the operation. This is known as surgical menopause.

Women are usually offered hormone replacement therapy (HRT) after a surgical menopause. This replaces some of the hormones normally produced by the ovaries. HRT is not suitable for everyone and some women experience side effects (see Appendix 2: Treatment)

Radiotherapy

Radiotherapy involves the use of high energy X-rays to destroy abnormal tissue, control symptoms, and shrink tumours. It can be applied outside the body using X-rays or within the body through drinking or injecting a liquid containing radioactive material.

Radiotherapy applied to the lower part of the abdomen in premenopausal women usually causes menopause. It can also cause the tissues in the vagina to become stiffer and less stretchy and give rise to vaginal dryness and pain during intercourse.

As with hysterectomy, doctors will usually offer HRT to help overcome the symptoms. They may also suggest lubricants and vaginal dilators.

Hormone Treatment for Cancer

Pre-menopausal women given hormone treatment for breast cancer are likely to experience menopause symptoms.

The treatment plan for breast cancer depends on the stage of the cancer and how far it has spread, the woman's general health and whether she has already gone through menopause.

Some breast cancers are affected by the female hormones, oestrogen and progesterone. Hormone therapy treatment lowers the amount of oestrogen in the body and blocks the action of oestrogen on breast cancer cells.

There are several types of hormonal therapy medicines including:

- aromatase inhibitors, (Arimidex, Aromasin, and Femara)
- selective oestrogen receptor modulators, (Tamoxifen, Evista, and Fareston)
- oestrogen receptor downregulators (Faslodex)

The dose and the period that it will need to be taken for depends on the individual and their response to the medication. Recent research has concluded that some women need to take Tamoxifen for up to ten years.

Appendix 2 Treatment for Menopause

Medical Options

1. Hormone Replacement Therapy (HRT)

HRT, also referred to as Hormone Therapy (HT), has been available since the 1930s.

Initially it was thought to be safe for women to start taking HRT at the onset of menopausal symptoms and to stay on it for the rest of their lives. Following the report of the Women's Health Initiative in 2002 it was recommended that women only stay on HRT for the short term (5 years) due to the potential health risks such as increased risk of heart attacks, blood clots, and breast cancer. The findings of the study have since been reviewed and revised.

Most women seek HRT to control hot flushes and night sweats but some also consider it because they think that it will help them to look and feel younger, and also give them more energy and a better sex drive. Research published in 2003 (NEJM, 2003) concluded that "In this trial in postmenopausal women, oestrogen plus progestin did not have a clinically meaningful effect on health-related quality of life".

As soon as hormone treatment stops menopause symptoms may recur regardless of age.

There is a large range of HRT products available, manufactured from a variety of ingredients. It can be administered in a variety of forms:

- Implants. A pellet containing a six-month supply of oestrogen is inserted under the skin of the lower abdomen.
- Tablets. This is the most common way of taking HRT where oestrogen is taken every day and progestogen is taken from day 15 to day 25 of the cycle.

- Skin patches. Skin patches deliver hormones directly to the blood-stream through the skin and, as with the implants, this means that the required dose is lower, reducing side effects.

- Vaginal rings, pessaries and creams. Preparations containing oestrogen to be applied directly to the vagina can be prescribed to ease symptoms such as vaginal dryness, itching, burning or discharge.

- Gels and creams. Oestrogen gels and creams rubbed on to the skin are absorbed easily and enter directly into the circulatory system.

Like any medication, HRT can have unpleasant side-effects including depression, skin rashes, hair loss, vomiting bloating and cystitis-like symptoms. It presents higher risks for some women particularly those who smoke, have high blood pressure, benign breast disease, endometriosis, pancreatitis, epilepsy or a family history of strokes.

2. Bio-Identical Hormone Replacement Therapy (BIHRT)

Bio-identical hormone therapy has been prescribed in the USA for many years and more recently has become available in the UK. It can be prescribed privately by specialist practitioners and on the NHS.

Bio-identical hormones have structures identical to human hormones and are mostly derived from plant sources including soy or Mexican yam root. Although they are considered to be 'more natural' than other HRT products, the plant compounds undergo synthetic processing to obtain the hormones used.

Common components of compounded bio-identical hormone formulations include estrone, estriol, testosterone, and micronized progesterone. There are bio-identical hormone products which are manufactured by big pharmaceutical companies, for example Crinone and Utrogest. These products undergo trials and testing in order to be approved by national health organisations such as the US Food and Drug Administration (FDA), the

UK Medicines and Healthcare products Regulatory Authority (MHRA) and the Australian Therapeutic Goods Administration (TGA).

Other BIHRT products are produced by compounding pharmacies according to the individual formulation of the prescribing practitioner. Practitioners prescribe a compound of hormones tailored to the needs of the individual, often based on the results of saliva and blood tests.

As with HRT, BIHRT can take a variety of forms including tablets and creams to suit different symptoms. Practitioners will normally aim to treat with the lowest dose for the shortest period of time.

3. Antidepressants

Some doctors prescribe antidepressants to lessen the effects of hot flushes and night sweats as well as for low mood and depression, particularly in cases where HRT is unsuitable or rejected. Antidepressants prescribed are mainly SSRI or SNRI which include Fluoxetine, Paroxetine, Citilopram, Escitalopram and Venlafaxine because these medications have a sedating effect.

It should be noted that antidepressants are not licensed for the management of menopausal hot flushes.

4. Sleeping Tablets

In the UK, more than 10 million prescriptions are written for sleeping pills every year. Medication offers only short-term relief because sleeping tablets treat the symptoms of poor sleep and not the causes. Medical practitioners are advised to prescribe drugs only after considering non-drug therapies

There are many over the counter sleep remedies available at a pharmacy. The common ingredient in all these pills is an antihistamine, which causes drowsiness.

Medical Practitioners may also prescribe medications for specific conditions such as: osteoporosis, under or over-active thyroid, diabetes and high blood pressure.

Complementary Approaches

For some women HRT is not suitable and many women prefer to pursue a complementary approach. To find a practitioner it is advisable to research a regulating organisation or an umbrella organisation such as Complementary and Natural Healthcare Council (CNHC).

The best complementary therapies are holistic, in that they treat the whole person. They can generally be used alongside medical treatment, but it is advisable to check with your medical practitioner if you are undergoing treatment.

When you are choosing a complementary therapist consider the following:

- Is the therapist qualified and insured?
- If you contact the therapist, do they welcome questions and answer them fully?
- Are they open about their fees?
- Do they have any testimonials on their website?

Be cautious about anyone who guarantees recovery or cures.

1. Mind/Body Techniques

i) Hypnotherapy

Hypnotherapy has been shown to be effective in helping women who experience hot flushes, particularly when hypnosis includes visualisation of cool images. Women can be taught self-hypnosis so that they can take control of their symptoms. Hypnosis recordings are also very effective.

Cognitive hypnotherapy brings together hypnotherapy with Neuro Linguistic Programming (NLP) techniques, positive psychology and elements of cognitive behaviour therapy to provide treatment that can target particular menopausal symptoms including poor sleep, weight gain and low mood.

UK http://www.cnhc.org.uk/pages/index.cfm

USA http://www.hypnotherapistregister.com

Cognitive Hypnotherapy www.questinstitute.co.uk

ii) Cognitive Behavioural Therapy (CBT)

CBT is based on the concept that your thoughts, feelings, physical sensations and actions are interconnected, and that negative thoughts and feelings can trap you in a vicious cycle. A CBT Practitioner will help you deal with overwhelming problems in a more positive way by breaking them down into smaller parts.

Research into the use of CBT in the management of hot flushes concluded that, 'A brief, unguided self-help CBT booklet is a potentially effective management option for working women experiencing problematic HFNS (hot flushes and night sweats).' Hardy, C., Griffiths, A., Norton, S., Hunter, M., *Self-help cognitive behaviour therapy for working women with problematic hot flushes and night sweats (MENOS@Work): a multicentre randomised controlled trial.*

UK https://www.cbtregisteruk.com/Default.aspx

USA http://www.nacbt.org/

iii) Meditation

Meditation has been shown to improve relaxation and reduce feelings of stress and anxiety. There are many books, apps and guided meditation recordings to enable women to meditate. Meditation instructors provide teaching and guidance to individuals and groups.

https://www.meditationinstructors.com/

2. Physical Therapies

i) Massage for Menopause

There are many types of massage such as Swedish, acupressure and aromatherapy. Treatments can ease stress, reduce fluid imbalance, alleviate headaches, and lessen muscle pains.

http://www.grcct.org/

ii) Reflexology

Reflexology is based on the principle that there are areas in the feet and hands that mirror each organ and structure in the body, and that they are connected to those organs by energy channels.

Regular reflexology treatments can support a woman going through menopause physically, mentally and emotionally by identifying imbalances and treating areas which need attention.

UK http://www.cnhc.org.uk/pages/index.cfm

USA http://reflexology-usa.org/

iii) Traditional Chinese Medicine (TCM)/Acupuncture

Acupuncture can be used to remove blockages or problems with the flow of energy around the body. Typically, an acupuncturist will formulate a treatment plan after talking to the client about her specific menopause symptoms, diet, lifestyle and overall health.

Traditional Chinese Medicine may also include taking herbal remedies.

UK www.acupuncture.org.uk

USA www.acupuncture.com

3. Herbal remedies

Herbal remedies can be purchased in chemists and food stores but for best effect it is advisable to consult a qualified herbalist.

Women taking herbal remedies should check the recommended period for taking them as many are only suitable for short term use. Women who are taking other medication or who seek medical treatment should tell their doctor if they are taking herbal remedies. https://nimh.org.uk/find-a-herbalist/

4. Other – homeopathy, aromatherapy, nutrition

i) Aromatherapy

Aromatherapy involves the use of essential oils to provide a range of therapeutic healing benefits. Aromatherapy oils can be administered by inhalation or they can be combined with massage to provide benefits that range from stimulating to relaxing, depending on the individual's symptoms and goals.

http://ifparoma.org/public/findatherapist.php

ii) Homeopathy

A range of homeopathic products can be purchased in chemists and food stores but for best effect it is advisable to consult a qualified homeopath. The appropriate remedy will depend on the constitution of the patient and how they are experiencing the symptoms.

UK http://www.homeopathy-soh.org

USA http://homeopathyusa.org/

iii) Nutrition

Food supplements can be useful in supporting health though the perimenopause, even for women who are eating a healthy, balanced diet. For advice and supplements that are tailored to your symptoms, consult a nutritionist.

UK http://www.findmynutritionist.co.uk/

USA http://www.findanutritionist.com/

Appendix 3 Clean Communication

Clean Communication is not about keeping the swearing out of your conversations! It is a technique that was developed in therapy to aid effective communication of issues and to elicit important information. It is a useful tool to use in conversations to enable the speaker to clarify the issues and to help the listener fully understand what is being said.

Many misunderstandings occur because we interpret what is being said from our own experience instead of finding out what the other person is trying to say. For example:

Sue: "I'm finding it difficult to cope with my hot flashes"

Dave: "So, you've got a problem with the sweating"

Sue: "I didn't think I sweated that much. What are you talking about? Has someone mentioned it to you?"

Dave: "No, I didn't mean that…."

Sue: "Well that's what you said. Now I feel even worse."

Does that sound familiar? A clean language way of approaching that conversation would be to reply using the words that Sue used.

Sue: "I'm finding it difficult to cope with my hot flashes"

Dave: (In a curious, interested tone) "Hmm. Coping with your hot flushes?"

Sue: "Yes. I feel really peculiar when my heart starts to thump"

Dave: "Your heart starts to thump and then what happens?"

Sue: "Well then I start to feel a bit dizzy and then the heat comes up from my chest all the way up to the top of my head"

Dave: "Up to the top of your head?"

Sue: "Yes. It feels good to be able to talk about it. I've been so worried".

This may sound a bit odd or contrived but it is surprising how much more understood the speaker feels and how much more information they give you.

The basic rules are:

- Listen carefully to what your colleague says
- Using a curious tone of voice, repeat back a few words
- If you need to ask a question do not introduce any of your own words, frame questions around the speaker's words for example: "And then what happens", "What kind of dizzy is that dizzy", "Is there anything else about that 'not coping'"

Using clean communication helps to build rapport, demonstrates that you are listening and reduces misunderstanding. It will help you colleague to express what she is feeling and will leave her feeling understood. It's a skill that is definitely worth practising.

Appendix 4 Making Reasonable Adjustments by Victoria Howell

As an employer, manager, equality and diversity, or HR professional you need to be aware of and follow the legislation and good practice to provide the right support to your workforce. You have a duty of care to all your employees' health and wellbeing at work.

People may not feel confident raising the topic of menopause with managers for fear of being judged or discriminated against. For example, a transgender man may not wish to disclose he is transgender and experiencing perimenopause symptoms. A woman in her 50's may not wish to disclose she has symptoms of perimenopause as she fears younger women may laugh about her. This is why awareness in your workplace needs to be aimed at all employees in addition to training and awareness for managers.

Consider this scenario:

You have been kept awake at night worrying about something at work, it is ruminating in your mind. You eventually fall asleep, only to be woken up by extreme stomach pain, hip soreness, and the feeling of being extremely hot and sweaty. You fall asleep for short periods of time during the night, only to be woken again. The alarm goes off for work and you are already tired. Imagine going through that most nights. How do you think you would feel?

It will not surprise you to consider how this can impact on your work life, feeling tired and groggy before the day begins. It can often lead to lack of concentration and can affect memory. Imagine yourself in a meeting feeling this way and being asked questions, that usually you would have no problem answering but due to the above, it is a problem for you. You feel embarrassed, and this will ultimately impact on your confidence to fulfil your role efficiently. You will be worried about what your colleagues and manager think of you.

Reasonable adjustments are for employees with disabilities or health conditions (ACAS). The Equality and Human Rights Committee say that "Equality Law recognised this may include changes to the way employment is structured. For example, removing barriers or providing extra support or resources". This is the Duty to make reasonable adjustments. Employers are responsible by law to provide a Duty of Care to all employees. The Law around reasonable adjustments is covered in more detail in Chapter .

So now you are aware of how the menopause can impact on a diverse age range of employees, how can you ensure you provide reasonable adjustments?

Your workplace environment

What type of culture does your workplace embrace? Do you have open values that all staff are encouraged to adhere to? Your values could include integrity, respect, trust, transparency, or support to name a few. Is your workforce aware of the values and do you practise these as a manager? Or are people afraid to confide in managers, afraid their issues will be discussed with other members of staff, or do they anticipate ridicule or discrimination?

Ensure you are approachable and professional. If staff do not trust you, they will not confide in you. Promote values of trust and excellence in your professional conduct. Raise the profile of an inclusive culture of wellbeing at work.

Training and awareness

You may include clauses relating to menopause in your existing employment policies or in a separate menopause policy. Creating a menopause policy, including menopause sickness, will assist accurate auditing, rather than generic gynaecological reasons for sickness (see Chapter 6).

Risk assess your work environment for people experiencing menopause symptoms, including a workstation assessment, as you would for mental health and pregnancy.

Hold menopause awareness sessions for all your employees.

Provide menopause awareness and support training for all managers. Provide them with a manager's menopause pack, which they can easily refer to when required.

You may wish to hire menopause specialist speakers/trainers if your workplace does not have the level of knowledge required. A trainer unknown to the workplace can help achieve better outcomes. They may also be able to offer 1-1 support for people experiencing problematic symptoms of the menopause, as part of an occupational health report recommendation.

The more that people in your company/corporation are aware of menopause, the further it will help eliminate the unnecessary taboo around this topic. People enduring menopause will feel better supported and more likely to share the problems that they encounter, which may impact on their ability to fulfil their job role.

Some reasonable adjustments to consider:

1. Provide a safe and confidential place to speak about symptoms, problems, and the impact it is having on the individual.

2. Workplace temperature – Hot flushes can occur any time, if possible, ask if the person would like to sit/work closer to an aircon unit, or an opening window.

3. Fans- provide fans at face and leg levels. During the peri menopause, and if the person is having irregular periods, the temperature will fluctuate too. During menstruation, body temperature is slightly raised, so that combined with hot flushes can make one feel incredibly uncomfortable and hot.

4. Anytime access to toilet facilities. For employees that travel to other sites or visit your site, make information available at the onset of their arrival to the whereabouts of the facilities. You could incorporate that into a welcome process for all, so people do not feel they are being singled out because of their peri menopause (or any other health condition, disability). Natural cooling sprays available in toilet facilities can help. Something with peppermint or other essential oils that help with cooling. These can be extremely effective.

5. Quiet space/room- somewhere undisturbed and safe for someone to go and deal with a hot flush or anxiety, dizzy spell or other symptoms necessitating a quiet place.

6. Uniforms - Review the composition of uniforms, are they made from natural fibres? Polyester and manmade fibre garments will contribute further to feeling hot and exacerbate a hot flush, causing sweat to drip and pool. Cotton or moisture wicking fabrics are readily available.

7. Cool water – There are inexpensive units that deliver fresh, cool water. These can be plumbed in so as not to run out. Other types are available via contract, where large bottles are provided as spares. When people are hydrated, it may help reduce the severity of hot flushes, it can also help enhance concentration levels.

8. Flexible working hours - People who have been awake during the night may need to start later, or prefer to start early, as they are already awake and prefer to finish earlier. Listen to what will work best for your employee. If the role permits, offer working from home.

9. Shower facilities - Many companies have shower facilities for staff, for example those who cycle into work and shower before starting their day. Awareness of facilities will be beneficial to those suffering extreme hot flushes, having a shower and change of clothes can

make all the difference to the ability to perform duties for the remainder of the day, instead of someone having to go home and lose a half day of work.

10. Private storage - When periods are irregular and unpredictable, maintain staff dignity and avoid embarrassment by providing somewhere private to store sanitary ware, change of clothes, deodorant and, or medication.

11. Vending machines – include healthier options like fruit, nuts and seeds.

12. Rest room - If work duties require long periods of sitting or standing, provide access to rest room.

Many of the above need to be in place for general mental and physical health requirements.

Consider the cost

The cost of making reasonable adjustments should be factored into the decision about what to implement. Many reasonable adjustments cost less than £100 or nothing at all. It may just require a change to an existing process or policy. Also, consider the costs of someone leaving and the advertising, recruitment, and training of a new person plus the impact this could have on a team adjusting and business.

By accommodating the needs of your current staff, staff will feel valued and engaged. Sickness and attrition will reduce, and your company will demonstrate an inclusive culture of valuing their staff. The corporate reputation will be one of excellence and this will engage the interest of further stakeholders and customers. You will have a clear return on investment and ability for succession planning, safe in the knowledge you are protecting your employees and your company and have delivered on your legal duty of care.

There are some factors that increase the risk of TDS for example, trauma to the testes and diabetes. Living an unhealthy lifestyle with poor diet, little exercise, alcohol abuse, and stress will also increase your chance of this condition.

There are tests and treatments available for TDS and if you are experiencing frequent or intense symptoms you should consult your medical practitioner.'

Appendix 6 Useful websites for Managers

Acas 'Challenging conversations and how to manage them' https://archive. acas.org.uk/conversations

BitC (2020) *Gender and Mental Health at Work* file:///C:/Users/patdu/ AppData/Local/Temp/bitc-factsheet-wellbeing-genderandmentalhealthat-work-july20.pdf

The British Menopause Society www.thebms.org.uk

CIPD *'A Practical Guide for People Managers',* https://www.cipd.co.uk/Im-ages/menopause-customisable-guide-for-people-managers_tcm18-55427. pdf

Faculty of Occupational Medicine of the Royal College of Physicians, Guidance on Menopause and the workplace. http://www.fom.ac.uk/ wp-content/uploads/Guidance-on-menopause-and-the-workplace-v6.pdf

Trade Unions Congress, The menopause in the workplace: A toolkit for trade unionists (2017) https://www.tuc.org.uk/sites/default/files/Meno-pause%20toolkit%20Eng%20FINAL.pdf

Unison The menopause is a workplace issue: guidance and model policy. https:// www.unison.org.uk/content/uploads/2019/10/25831.pdf

University of Nottingham, *Work and the Menopause: A guide for Managers*, 2020 https://www.nottingham.ac.uk/hr/guidesandsupport/equalityanddi-versitypolicies/documents/work-and-the-menopause-a-guide-for-manag-ers.pdfThe Job Accommodation Network, a free consulting service of the Office of Disability Employment Policy, the U.S. Department of Labor, has an extremely useful website with numerous fact-sheets suggesting rea-sonable adjustments ("accommodation" in the USA) on http://askjan.org

For Book Bonuses http://www.patduckworth.com/menopausemindthegap

Appendix 7 Useful Websites for Employees

Daisy Network providing information and support to women diagnosed with Premature Ovarian Insufficiency, also known as Premature Menopause. https://www.daisynetwork.org

Henpicked is a website for women over 40, providing articles about menopause and other midlife issues. https://henpicked.net/

International Menopause Society (2020) *Premature ovarian insufficiency: An International Menopause Society White Paper* https://www.tandfonline.com/doi/full/10.1080/13697137.2020.1804547

The Menopause Exchange www.menopause-exchange.co.uk

Menopause Matters www.menopausematters.co.uk

Menopause Support UK www.menopausesupport.co.uk/

My Menopause Doctor www.menopausedoctor.co.uk

NHS menopause pages www.nhs.uk/Conditions/Menopause/Pages/Symptoms.aspx

NHS information on HRT www.nhs.uk/Conditions/Hormone-replacement-therapy/Pages/Introduction.aspx

NICE Menopause: diagnosis and management www.nice.org.uk/guidance/ng23Healthtalk.orgwww.healthtalk.org/peoples-experiences/later-life/menopause/topics

Women's Health Concerns www.womens-health-concern.org/help-and-advice/factsheets/focus-series/menopause

For Book Bonuses http://www.patduckworth.com/menopausemindthegap

Appendix 8 Books

Cool Recipes for Hot Women: How to eat your way to a healthy menopause by Pat Duckworth with Jenny Tschiesche (2014)

Hot Women; Cool Solutions: How to manage menopause symptoms using mind/body techniques by Pat Duckworth (2012)

How to Survive Her Menopause: A practical guide to women's health for men', by Pat Duckworth (2013)

Employment Law - An Adviser's Handbook by Tamara Lewis Published Legal Action Group. Edition 12 (2017)

Book Bonuses

Go to http://www.patduckworth.com/menopausemindthegap for book bonuses including:

- Live Webinar - Menopause Basics
- Video – Early Menopause Experience interview with Lesley Fettes
- PDF – Menopause Symptoms Factsheet
- PDF - "Why & how to check your vulva" by Victoria Howell
- 50% off 28 Day Hormone Reset Programme with Personal Trainer Jackie Grant
- Re-ignite Your Passion Coaching with Jill McCulloch

Acknowledgements

It takes a village to raise a book and I am fortunate to have so many amazing people in my personal village.

Thank you to all my Evolutionary Business Council friends who have supported me during the writing and publishing process. In no particular order: Ben Gioia, Christine Powers, Lisa Dadd, Dr Lin Morel, Teresa de Grosbois, Dr Wini Curley and Sarah Ross.

Many thanks to Gary Stuart for his wonderful work with me on the title.

I am grateful to Jill McCulloch, Victoria Howell, Lesley Fettes and Hannah Caulfield for their contributions which enrich the book.

Thank you to Christine Koetsier for your soul encouragement during this challenging year.

As always, thanks to Kay Newton for keeping me sane and making me laugh. 'Don't get me started…!'

Thank you to my husband, Alex Duckworth, for your patience and support during a challenging 2020.

About the Author

Pat Duckworth is a Women's Wellbeing Strategist, Author and International Public Speaker. After over 30 years working in the public and voluntary sector at a Senior Management Level, Pat retrained as a therapist and coach. She has published four books including the Award-winning 'Hot Women, Cool Solutions: How to control menopause symptoms using mind/body techniques.' Her fourth book, 'Hot Women Rock: How to discover your midlife entrepreneurial mojo', became a #1 International Best Seller.

Pat advises organisations who are committed to supporting women colleagues at menopause on strategies for managing physical, mental and emotional symptoms. She has delivered workshops for HMRC, Office of National Statistics, NHS, ASP, Cambridge Academic Partnerships and Cheshire Fire Service.

The combination of Pat's personal knowledge of menopause combined with her many hours of clinical work and management experience means that she is well placed to understand the needs of female employees and their employers.